Dialectical Behavior Therapy

The Ultimate Guide for Using DBT for Borderline Personality Disorder, Difficult Emotions, and Mood Swings, Including Techniques such as Mindfulness and Emotion Regulation

Contents

INTRODUCTION 1
   DBT ORIGINS: MARSHA LINEHAN 1
   DBT IS NOT 3
   DBT IS 4

CHAPTER ONE: DBT & BORDERLINE PERSONALITY DISORDER 5

CHAPTER TWO: DBT & DIFFICULT EMOTIONS AND MOOD SWINGS 9

CHAPTER THREE: MINDFULNESS 11
   What Does Mindfulness Consist of? 11
   USING THE WHAT SKILLS 11
      Observe 11
      Describe 17
      Participate 20
   USING THE HOW SKILLS 30
      Nonjudgmentally 30
      One-Mindfully 37
      Effectively 39

CHAPTER FOUR: DISTRESS TOLERANCE 42

USING CRISIS SURVIVAL: DISTRACTION WITH WISE MIND 42

- *A – Activities* 42
- *C – Contributing* 42
- *C – Comparison* 44
- *E – Emotions* 44
- *P – Pushing Away* 45
- *T – Thoughts* 45
- *S – Sensations* 46

USING SELF-SOOTHE WITH THE FIVE SENSES 47

- *Taste* 48
- *Smell* 48
- *See or Vision* 48
- *Hear* 49
- *Touch* 49
- *Sensory Wrap Up* 50

CHAPTER FIVE: USING I.M.P.R.O.V.E. THE MOMENT 51

- *I – Imagery* 51
- *M – Meaning* 53
- *P – Prayer* 53
- *R – Relaxation* 54
- *O – One Thing at a Moment* 55
- *V – Vacation* 56
- *E – Encouragement* 57

I.M.P.R.O.V.E. SKILLS WRAP-UP 57

PROS AND CONS 57

CHAPTER SIX: USING ACCEPTING REALITY 61

WILLINGNESS 61

WILLFULNESS 61

TURNING OF THE MIND 62
RADICAL ACCEPTANCE 63

CHAPTER SEVEN: EMOTION REGULATION 66

P & L – Treating Physical Illnesses 66
E – Balanced Eating 67
A – Avoid Mood-Altering Drugs 67
S – Balanced Sleep 68
E – Get Exercise 68
USING MASTERY 68
BUILD POSITIVE EXPERIENCES 69
Short Term 69
Long Term 73
POSITIVE MINDFULNESS 76
Be Mindful of Positive Emotions 77
Using the Opposite to Emotion Action 77

CHAPTER EIGHT: INTERPERSONAL EFFECTIVENESS 80

USING OBJECTIVENESS EFFECTIVENESS (D.E.A.R. M.A.N.) 80
D – Describe 80
E – Express 81
A – Assert 81
R – Reinforce 82
M – Mindful (stay) 83
A – Appear Confident 84
N – Negotiate 84
D.E.A.R. M.A.N. 86
USING RELATIONSHIP EFFECTIVENESS (G.I.V.E.) 87
G – (be) Gentle 87
I – (act/be) Interested 88
V – Validate 89

    E – (use an) Easy Manner *89*

SELF-RESPECT EFFECTIVENESS (F.A.S.T.) 90

    F – Fair *90*

    A – (no) Apologies *91*

    S – Stick to Your Values *91*

    T – (be) Truthful *92*

T.H.I.N.K. 92

    T – Think *92*

    H – Have empathy *93*

    I – Interpretations *93*

    N – Notice *93*

    K – Kindness *94*

CONCLUSION **95**

Introduction

DBT Origins: Marsha Linehan

Dialectical behavior therapy is a fairly recent therapy. It emerged in the 1980s as an evidence-based, goal-oriented therapy and was originally developed as a modified form of cognitive behavioral therapy. It was intended to treat patients with borderline personality disorder. It has since been proven effective for patients who suffer other mental illnesses – such as depression, anxiety, self-harm, traumatic brain injuries, PTSD, chemical dependency, and distress from sexual abuse. It has also been proven effective for a branch of PTSD called C-PTSD, or complex post-traumatic stress disorder, when you're born into a situation that you don't realize is abuse much later.

Marsha Linehan, a psychology professor at the University of Washington, founded DBT largely based on Buddhist meditative practices. Studies have shown that DBT has a higher retention rate among clients and a lower suicide rate than other forms of therapy for the range of mental illnesses listed above.

She began the therapy after noticing a "burn-out" among colleagues with chronic suicidal patients. She noticed that these patients primarily came from homes that were not very nurturing and supportive and thus needed continual external validation well into their adult lives.

Patients who come from these backgrounds are prime examples of C-PTSD survivors. They are used to having their feelings invalidated and their voices squashed. Linehan developed a type of therapy where the therapist is viewed as an ally rather than an adversary – and validates the patient's feelings – while at the same time, pointing out where their behavior might be maladaptive and coming to better solutions together.

The ultimate goal of DBT is for the client to "have a life worth living" – whatever healthy frame the patient decides that is. DBT uses both acceptance and change where it is the healthiest fit. Linehan's model is novel in the sense that it changes the role of the therapist from authority figure to a team member, based on intersubjective tough love.

Dialectical behavior therapy offers four components that interplay with each other to create the best learning environment for the client.

- Individual – the therapist and the client discuss issues that have come up during the week. This can be broken down into priorities with each client and may vary depending on the week:
    o Self-harm, suicidal ideation, or plans to hurt others take first priority.
    o Therapy-interfering behaviors are second priority. These can come from either the therapist or the client and include issues such as being late, forgetting to pay, canceling, not doing homework, passive or aggressive behaviors, non-compliance, or personality clashes.
    o Tertiary – the quality of life issues take priority. This is where the therapist and the client discuss issues

such as work, family, social life, and working towards improving the skills learned.
- Groups generally meet once a week for two sessions. These sessions run for two and a half hours and clients learn to use the specific skills DBT is comprised of, which are as follows:
    - Core mindfulness
    - Interpersonal effectiveness
    - Emotion regulation
    - Distress tolerance
- Therapist consultation team – this team consists of all the DBT therapists in the facility working together to support the therapists providing the treatment.
- Phone coaching – this is brief and focuses on the skills learned in individual and group sessions to help the client better focus on daily life.

No component is used by itself. The individual sessions are used to build a better rapport with the clients and keep suicidal or emotional outbursts from interrupting a group. On the other hand, group sessions are used to apply the techniques learned. The therapist consultation team is used to keep the team up-to-date on how clients are doing and if they should look out for a behavior in a group – as well as keep the therapists' morale up and support each other. The phone coaching is used for limited circumstances and would be fairly pointless without individual and group sessions.

DBT Is Not

In talk therapy, many people are wary of therapists because they do not allow the patient to come to his or her own conclusions. Instead, they may offer very heavy "suggestions", which any serious-minded patient will do. What works for one patient does not always work for another, no matter how the therapist may have been practicing.

Talk therapy also heavily relies on Sigmund Freud. While he may have pioneered psychology as we know it today, and we would not know to separate different parts of the brain without his work, Freudian therapists look for a root cause to problems, and many root causes, according to Freudian psychology, relate back to sex or sexual desire or sexual organs, or sex in some manner.

However, not everything is about sex, and it was ironically Freud who uttered the now famous line, "Sometimes a cigar is just a cigar." This would lead a true Freudian psychologist to believe that he is hiding (and not well) his blatant homosexual desires by seeing a phallic symbol for everyone else but brushing it off as a cigar for himself.

Less is known about the yonic symbol – that of the female sexual desire, and in the shape of a triangle – because women were not supposed to enjoy sex in his time, nor were men supposed to treat women as anything *other* than a sex symbol. Not much has changed.

DBT Is

Dialectical behavior therapy is research and evidence-based therapy, somewhat new in the field of therapeutics. It incorporates talk therapy, which is the most common form of therapy, wherein the patient simply talks about his or her problems and comes to a conclusion. A good therapist does more listening than talking and allows the patient to reach conclusions on his or her own. A good therapist will bring the discussion back to the topic when the patient goes off on tangents, and allow the patient to reach conclusions and modify their behavior as they see fit, with some directional input from the therapist.

It began as CBT, or cognitive behavioral therapy, and branched off from there, combining distress tolerance and spiritual awareness. It began – and is largely used today – to treat borderline personality patients. It is also helpful in treating patients prone to self-harm, anxiety, depression, and PTSD from sexual trauma.

Chapter One: DBT & Borderline Personality Disorder

How can DBT treat borderline personality disorder or BPD? To start, let's define BPD. The National Institution of Mental Health describes BPD as a disorder affecting the mood, which can cause extreme anxiety, anger, or depression – lasting for several hours or several days. This is different from bipolar disorder, which is a manic-depressive disorder, causing unusual shifts in energy, mood, and ability to carry out daily activities. Bipolar disorder must be medicated, whereas BPD may be treated with counseling and meditation.

BPD is marked by varying patterns of self-image, mood, and behavior. It includes fears of abandonment, either real or imagined, some of which may lead to a self-fulfilling prophecy, unstable relationships, and feelings of emptiness. Treatment is more helpful than medication in treating depression, anger, and self-harm in individuals with BPD.

A borderline personality disorder is very common – over 3 million people have been diagnosed with it. It was named as such since the people diagnosed with it were thought to be "on the border" of diagnoses of psychosis and neurosis.

Finding online support groups for BPD tends to be very difficult. Borderline personality disorder, like many other mental illnesses, is difficult and embarrassing to admit – and it is on a spectrum. Someone who occasionally feels empty and fears abandonment may be considered borderline, while it could also go to the end of the spectrum and be borderline schizophrenic. Many support groups offer support if you have a BPD spouse. It tends to affect women more than men for some reason. Many support groups are designed for the boyfriends/husbands/girlfriends/wives of people with it. Few groups are designed for those with the actual diagnosis. It's great that their support system has somewhere to go for help. For those diagnosed with BPD, self-help may not be the most ideal solution. This is where dialectical behavior therapy comes in.

DBT works with both the individual and the group therapy. This is reassuring for several reasons. Primarily, the individual therapy, like any mental illness, is necessary so that the patient feels heard. The group therapy is especially important in DBT because this is where they learn to utilize the skills. DBT is all about interpersonal relationships. Without the opportunity to practice the skills in an interpersonal setting, the skills are just theory and therefore somewhat useless. The theory may well be fascinating, but it only works on paper – like Marxism. Once you add human beings to the mix, shit gets real.

Dialectical behavior therapy is not the only therapy used to treat BPD. It has just been proven to be the most effective. Mentalization-based therapy (MBT) is a talk therapy designed to help people identify and understand what others might be thinking and feeling.

The main reason this is less effective is that we have no way of knowing what's going on inside someone else's head – and frankly, it's none of our business. Many people might say, "I don't care what anyone thinks." That line is bull. Everyone cares. What someone thinks of you directly affects how they treat you, and *everyone* cares about that. However, the axiom that what others think about is none of your business is true. You can pretend not to care about it, or you can admit that you do, but at the end of the day, it's still none of your business, and there is *no way* to know what someone else is thinking.

Secondly, we have no control over someone else's thoughts or actions, so spending time talking about them is a fairly pointless endeavor. We can control only our own actions. We can't even control our own thoughts. We can make a concerted effort to think about something else, but in trying *not* to think about something, we think more about it. Thoughts aren't like ants marching in a straight line, easily discernable one from the next. They're more like ants swarming on a cookie, completely indiscernible from each other and not entirely in our control – but we can control our actions.

Transference-focused therapy (TFT) is used to help clients understand their emotions and interpersonal issues through the relationship they build with their therapist, and then they learn to apply those skills to other people.

This therapy is less effective because patients and therapists will never have an equal relationship. A patient is supposed to walk into a therapist's office and mentally strip down naked in front of a complete stranger. If the patient knows that much about the therapist, the therapist has certainly crossed the line of professionalism. Because of the wall of professionalism, a patient/therapist relationship will *never* be equal. Because of this inequality, whatever skills the client has learned here are somewhat diluted in the real world, where relationships are not automatically an authority figure setting.

Good Psychiatric Management (GPM) provides a sort of "tool-kit" for therapists to adopt and use for clients with severe mental illnesses. This therapy sort of works as a cherry picker from all other forms of therapy to adapt to individual clients.

This is a decent form of therapy, but more difficult to set goals and outlines. It also doesn't offer group therapy specifically, which is necessary for individuals with BPD.

Medications are often used as a Band-Aid for BPD. They can't cure it. They can help with other mental illnesses that individuals with BPD usually have, like depression, anxiety, or PTSD. Even with those mental illnesses, therapy is encouraged.

Self-help is encouraged for all people with mental illnesses, and those who have not been diagnosed with any (they probably have some. Who doesn't?). Self-help includes things like sleeping, hydrating, exercising, socializing, doing activities you enjoy, and getting alone time.

DBT is most effective for BPD because it focuses on the present moment, the present emotion. The concept of mindfulness teaches skills to control the present emotion, self-harm, and impulsivity. DBT is a proactive and problem-solving approach designed specifically for BPD.

DBT uses a one-on-one approach with a therapist who is trained to be less of an authority figure and more of a teammate, as well as groups that are designed to help people learn how to use interpersonal skills.

However, because it has been found to be so effective, it is used for other mental illnesses as well. Mental illnesses all tend to overlap somewhere. There is no mental illness in a vacuum.

Chapter Two: DBT & Difficult Emotions and Mood Swings

On the surface, BPD can look like bipolar, but as stated, they are different disorders. The same can be said for difficult emotions and mood swings. That is a very vague description of mental illnesses, as all emotions can be difficult. Also, all people have mood swings to a degree.

However, for people with emotional dysregulation, DBT has been proven to help manage extreme emotions, including repression of feelings, which often leads to confusion and shame of emotions. The patient may not know what he or she feels and feels guilty for feeling it. When it comes to emotions, there is no "should". They just *are*.

DBT treats BPD and difficult emotions and mood swings by teaching emotion regulation, holding the patient accountable for their actions, allowing the patient to feel what they feel, and redirecting self-harm behaviors into something productive. Self-harm is not isolated to only cutting. It could include excessive sex, binge eating, starving oneself, excessive spending, extreme laziness, eating only junk food, self-isolating, and more.

By teaching mindfulness, distress tolerance, emotion regulation, and interpersonal effectiveness, DBT utilizes skills and strategies that help the client overcome harmful emotions and associated behaviors.

DBT has been shown to be effective for reducing suicidal ideation, non-suicidal self-harm, psychiatric hospitalization, treatment dropout, substance abuse, and improving global functioning.

Retention rate is difficult to maintain in any type of therapy. When it starts getting hard for people, right when they are getting close to a breakthrough, they often drop out. DBT holds people accountable for that. It also has a clear outline that patients can see regarding how close they are to finishing treatment. This clear outline helps people feel less overwhelmed – like there's no end in sight and that they can't get better. If there's seemingly an end in sight, it's been proven that people will work harder to reach that goal.

Chapter Three: Mindfulness

Mindfulness plays an integral part in DBT. Mindfulness means paying attention to what is happening right now – and doing so on purpose. By "on purpose" we mean choosing to be in the moment. If you are at a comedy club, for example, and the comedian is entertaining, you'll be paying attention to him or her. That is not mindfulness – you are not *deliberately* in the moment.

What Does Mindfulness Consist of?

Mindfulness is having a wise mind and being present in the moment. There are many facets to being mindful. It consists of observing, describing, and participating in the present moment. What does it mean to do these things? It means not to let your mind wander. Bring it back to the present moment.

Even if you don't have BPD, or any diagnosed mental illness, learning mindfulness and learning how to live in the present moment and notice everything about this particular moment without worrying about the future or the past is a useful skill for anyone to have.

Using the What Skills

Observe

One facet of mindfulness is that of observation. A mindful person observes his or her surroundings. Think like a spy or a fraud psychic.

Like *Burn Notice* or *Psyche* or *Monk*. The main characters of those shows are hyper-observant. They notice details the average person would miss, which is why they're fictional characters.

In real life, however, an average person can still be mindful without solving crimes in their sleep. The type of observation that is necessary for mindfulness is, quite simply stated, observing the present. However, because mindfulness *is* the psychological process of bringing one's attention to the present, that definition is rather redundant.

To get a deeper understanding of why observation is necessary for mindfulness, we must first understand what it is we are to observe, and why it is necessary.

Mindfulness in any degree relies heavily on emotions, or the lack thereof. Because we are discussing mindfulness in the context of DBT, we will discuss mostly emotion or the lack thereof.

Let's first discuss lack of emotion. To simply lack an emotion is not mindfulness. That is the opposite of mindfulness because it creates apathy or emptiness, both of which are numb states of being.

The lack of emotion in mindfulness is closer to having reached a state of nirvana, wherein you feel calm and peaceful. While calm and peaceful *are* emotions, they are much less intrusive emotions than most others, including the actual lack of emotions, such as apathy and emptiness, as we've discussed.

Apathy or emptiness often results in being on autopilot, which is the *opposite* of mindfulness. Mindfulness is a deliberate state of being. Think, for example, your drive home from a familiar place. Your mind wanders, you maybe think about what you're going to make for dinner or why Billy's teacher is calling you, or that excellent comeback you should've said to Susan at work. *Man, she's annoying!* You're on autopilot. There are days you wondered if your car didn't drive itself home because you don't remember how you got there.

Autopilot is useful. It saves time and energy. It helps us become good at what we do. If a basketball player, for example, has to think about dribbling and running, he or she will make a horrible player. Instead, they run on autopilot. They are not being mindful of the present moment because they have to think about the whole game. Whose skills are best utilized for what? Who's going to catch this pass? Who's going to make the shot? Who's going to pass it to someone who is?

Autopilot is an extremely useful part of our everyday lives. If you suffered a traumatic brain injury or autoimmune disease which makes you forget everything, you might have to literally teach yourself how to walk again. You're now forced to be in the moment. You have to think, *Lift your right leg. Put it down in front of you. Now the left. Don't forget to breathe.*

If we had to think about things as simple as walking all the time, we wouldn't get anything done. TBI's and chronic illnesses sort of force people to be mindful.

But what about *choosing* to be mindful? This is where you choose to observe the world around you, your emotions, and other people's emotions. Observing is *just* noticing, not thinking or analyzing. *I am feeling sad. I am feeling content. I am feeling angry.* Don't wonder why; just notice. *That person is smiling as if they're happy. That person is scowling as if they're angry. That person has no outward emotional facial expression as if they're content.* Since you can't actually *know* what someone is feeling, you take an educated guess based on body language at face value.

Observing is sort of a check-in point. We check in with what we are feeling. When we observe, we contact. We make contact with the present moment. When we think, we distance. We distance ourselves from the present moment even if we are thinking *about* the present moment. For example, *Why am I happy?* is a thought that takes us away from the present moment of simply *being* happy. We wonder what has happened or will happen to make us so, which puts us in the past or future. But *I am happy* is just noticing, observing, and making contact with the present moment without analyzing it.

When we observe and check in, we are more apt to make better decisions for ourselves. We check in with our bodies and realize we need food or rest. We check in with our sensations and notice or realize that we need external stimulation or silence. We check in with our thoughts and are better able to make more correct decisions for ourselves, at this moment.

Observing is just noticing and checking in. Sounds pretty simple, right? But how often do we actually do that? When you're watching TV, for example, are you watching it, or is it more white noise while you do other things? Human beings have become so adept at multitasking that we almost don't even realize we're doing it anymore.

Autopilot and multitasking have evolved over the years and have added layers of protection to our psyches. If we were mindful of every single thing we did, firstly, we wouldn't get anything done. Secondly, it would be exhausting to be that conscientious of everything.

However, in the realm of DBT, the *Observe* aspect of mindfulness is extremely helpful. It is this aspect that allows us to slow down for a moment and look at our lives as if we're looking at puzzle pieces before we look at the whole. We're not even thinking, *Where does this blue corner piece go?* We're thinking, *Here is a piece. It is blue. It is shaped like a corner.* It may feel frustrating to *know* it belongs in the corner but to have to slow down and just observe *that* it is a corner piece. However, like math, DBT works best if you don't skip steps.

For DBT novices – or even professionals – the best place to start observing lies in your breathing. *I am inhaling. I am exhaling. I feel the rise and fall of my chest. I am inhaling deeper. I am holding my breath. I am exhaling slower. Now I feel the rise and fall of my stomach.* When you focus on your breathing like that, you are forced to focus on the present. When you feel your mind wandering, you can just bring it back to your breathing.

Observing is all about staying in the present. You can also observe your other senses.

I feel cool wind on my face. I feel the sun on my face. I feel the perfect temperature of an air-conditioned office building on my face.

Move on to other body parts, other sensations. But remember, this is all about noticing, not judging, fixing, or even thinking about it. Just noticing.

I feel the pressure of my seat against my legs, bottom, and back. I am touching the couch with my fingertips. I feel a hole in my sock.

However, don't get distracted by the hole. Carry on. Notice.

You may want to do a full body scan.

I feel my heart beating. I feel the denim against my legs. I feel my calf muscles twitch. I feel my stomach rumble.

When you've noticed everything about and around you that you can feel without getting up and touching anything, start noticing sounds.

I hear the air conditioner. I hear the clock. I hear the traffic. I hear a dog barking. I hear my stomach growling. I hear the TV.

When a sound arises in your mind, listen to it. Notice it. Then move on.

Move on to another sense.

I see a door. I see a man in a red jacket. I see a wet floor sign.

Again, notice, but do not judge. Do not spend time on any one image – just long enough to notice it.

I see a TV. I see fried chicken. I see two people talking.

Don't stop to watch the TV, or listen to the conversation, or eat the chicken. Just notice that they are all there.

Move on to taste, without actually eating.

I taste the remnants of my toothpaste. I taste the filling from the dentist appointment this morning.

This is a much harder sense to observe – unless you are physically eating something.

Observe any smells in the vicinity.

I smell that fried chicken.

Refrain from eating someone else's fried chicken, no matter how good it smells or looks.

I smell cigarette smoke. I smell babies.

They have a specific smell, although it's hard to describe. Please refrain from eating babies too, no matter how good they smell.

I smell rain. I smell a construction crew repaving the road.

The "sixth sense" is thought. Notice your thoughts come and go. Do not cling to, or actively avoid any of them. Like feelings, they are neither good nor bad. They just *are*.

Observation is experiential. That is, it must be experienced. It cannot be learned through discussion or books or even movies.

To observe is *not* to label. Just notice. Notice with your "wise mind" or the place where your reasonable mind and your emotional mind overlap. It's difficult as humans not to label things because language is tied up so intricately with thought and memory.

This book, or any other, cannot describe what we're seeing *without* labeling it because to convey messages to another requires the use of words, and therefore labels.

Yet, in practice, in your wise mind, you don't need words. You just need to use your senses to discover the world around you. You may be tempted to "zone out", or may even do so on accident. However, that would be counterproductive to mindfulness.

Mindfulness isn't just being presently there. It's all about being there in the present. Doing so opens us up to the wise mind. When the emotional mind and the rational mind overlap, you just *know* something is true. You don't have any fear or anxiety about it.

The wise mind is that "aha" moment, often felt in the gut. Your brain might lead you astray. Your heart will, on at least occasion, lead you astray. Your libido will definitely lead you astray. However, your gut will not lead you astray. When you have to talk yourself into or out of a decision, it usually "feels" wrong. If you don't have to talk yourself into or out of a decision, but just *know* it is right, that is the wise mind. That is the "aha" moment.

People reach the wise mind at different stages and because of different triggers. It is not something that is reached once and then forgotten about. Our emotional minds and our rational minds have an ongoing struggle. When they come to an agreement, it is a wise mind place of negotiation. We may have several of these moments a day, or we may only have several in a lifetime.

Describe

Describing is the next step in mindfulness. In the *Observe* section, the book does describe this to a degree because it must use language. Your brain, however, need not describe something in order just to notice it.

Take an activity that may not be pleasurable to you, for example again, washing dishes. In the last section, we sort of "zoned out" during the dishwashing because it simply had to get done. In this section, let's describe everything about the activity, without focusing on feelings.

The water is hot. This plate is slippery. There is some gunk stuck to this dish. The dish soap smells good.

Describing is another skill set used to help us stay in the present. It is also useful to apply verbal labels to feelings. In the *Observe* section, we noticed that we were happy. Again, because we need words to communicate via writing, we used the *word* happy.

In this section, <u>allow</u> your brain to use the words.

I am happy. I am upset.

We can even go into further detail about *why* we are feeling such things.

I am happy I got to see my niece. I am upset my client canceled at the last minute.

When we get in the habit of describing simple tasks, such as washing the dishes, or feelings such as happiness or being upset, we are better able to both communicate and manage our emotions and our day-to-day lives.

Emotions and facts, however, are not always synonymous. For example, a rape survivor may hear an accent similar to that of her rapist and feel afraid, but she is not in any present danger. The mind reacts to past triggers and events as if it were in the present.

While this presents an added complication to anxiety or PTSD patients, coming back to the *actual* present, being mindful, helps to reduce the perceived danger.

Your anxiety may present the thought, *No one likes me, or I am unlovable.* These are just thoughts though, and thoughts are not always fact. Because every person's thoughts first must filter through layers, "facts" are often subjective. There do exist, in reality, some completely objective facts. While these facts are presented in the form of thoughts, everything is presented in the form of thoughts; thus, negating the validity of many thoughts.

Describe your thoughts in conjunction with what is going on around you and inside of you to assess better if the thoughts are facts or not.

I am going to fail this exam, is just a thought. Describe your body. Do you have sweaty palms? An upset stomach? Even if these things are true, it still may not be "fact" that you're going to fail because you don't know yet. If you switch your thinking to, *I am going to pass this exam,* you still may have the sweaty palms and upset stomach. It is still just a thought, neither true nor untrue because the future is an unknown variable.

Bring your mindset back to the present. Describe what you're feeling in the present tense. *I feel anxious about the upcoming exam.* Notice your surroundings. Are your palms sweaty? Do you have an upset stomach? The statement in the present tense is more likely to be accurate and easier to ascertain accuracy.

Take the thought again, *No one likes me.* That is present tense. What descriptions corroborate or contradict this thought? Whom do you mean when you say no one? Do people actively avoid you? This thought is harder to claim or denounce as fact because it's impossible to know what's going on in someone else's head.

When you describe an event or a feeling without judgment, it may become apparent to you that the thoughts and experiences are separate from each other. That's not to say the thoughts and experiences aren't real. They are very real. The feelings they represent are very real. The thoughts and feelings may be about an experience in the past that's triggering thoughts and feelings in the present. Those thoughts and feelings are still real. You may have thoughts and feelings related to an experience that never happened in reality. Those thoughts and feelings are still real.

"It's all in your head" is something ignorant people say when they don't want to discuss something. Technically, everything is "all in our heads" as that is where the brain is located. Other people may dismiss your thoughts and feelings as invalid. If you do the same, you're left with no footing on which to assess them.

Thoughts, feelings, and experiences are all valid and unique. Two identical twins could have the same experience and have completely different feelings about it because they've led different lives; they have different pasts from which to draw conclusions.

Two people could have experienced the same event and have totally different experiences. For example – and this is controversial, but it's based on fact and life experience –, an American woman went through a Holocaust museum once with another woman who'd been raised in Berlin. The American woman felt physically sick at the end, whereas the German woman was not phased at all because she'd been taught since birth that the Holocaust never happened and Americans built the museum to make Germany look bad. The two women had totally different experiences of the same event because they'd had different life experiences and education.

We are made up of our memories, even the memories we've forgotten. No two people have the same life experiences in the same time frames. Ergo, all thoughts, feelings, and experiences are valid and unique.

Some countries teach that there are five continents, depending on where the line break is in the land. Some countries teach that there are seven. Neither teaching is invalid. One may be wrong. Or they both may be wrong, and the answer is six. The Earth is constantly shifting and changing. Who knows?

That said, thoughts, feelings, and experiences are not altogether the same things. A thought is not the same as a feeling, and neither of those is the same as the experience.

If you can describe all of them separately, you will be better able to separate ideas from facts and be better able to communicate to others what is happening or has happened, how you feel or felt about it, and why one event leads to a particular thought.

Participate

There are a variety of mindful exercises to practice either in group therapy or individual. Some of these exercises can be practiced on your own, without therapy, although therapy is recommended since that is the topic of this book. Furthermore, it's recommended because it's been proven to work.

Exercises in Participation:

- *The Raisin Exercise*

    This works well with any type of food that has an interesting texture, taste, or smell.

This is better equipped for group therapy. The facilitator produces raisins to a group of eight-twelve people and instructs them to individually describe the object, on the premise that they've never seen a raisin before. They can't describe it saying, "It's a raisin," or even "It's a dried grape," because the premise is they know nothing about raisins.

This exercise brings the clients into the present moment. "It's wrinkly," or "It tastes kind of like a grape," are acceptable responses from someone who's never seen a raisin before.

This exercise forces them to notice everything about the raisin and say something that hasn't been said already. When their mind is occupied, they can't be ruminating on the worries and stressors that usually consume their time. They are forced into the present moment.

When you follow these instructions and pay close attention to the object in front of you and the people around you, you are practicing mindfulness. You are deliberately being in the present moment.

- *The Body Scan*

    In this exercise, the clients lie on the floor with their feet slightly apart or sit on a chair with their backs straight and their feet on the floor. If they are lying down, their palms are facing up. The facilitator asks the participants to close their eyes.

    The facilitator then asks the clients to stay very still and move with awareness only when needed to shift positions. Pretend you're getting an MRI done. That kind of non-movement. If you have involuntary twitches, it won't disrupt anything in this exercise, unlike the MRI.

    The facilitator brings the clients' attention to their breathing. They're not asked to change their breathing patterns in any way, but just to notice them. Clients may realize they're not breathing as deeply as they should be. Participants may change their breathing style without being aware, but either changing involuntarily or not changing is not important. What's important is noticing. Do you breathe through your nose or mouth? Do you exhale through your nose or your mouth? Do you feel your stomach or chest rise and fall? What is the rhythm of your breathing? Just notice these things, without doing anything about them.

The facilitator then brings attention to the body and how things feel in contact with it. Notice how your clothes feel against your skin. Notice the pressure of your body against the floor. Notice the temperature in the room. Again, do nothing about these things, just notice them.

The facilitator then asks the participants to notice how the body feels in and of itself. Notice the beating of your heart. Notice any parts of your body that feel weak or strong, heavy or light. Notice if any part of your body is numb or tingly or in pain, or feels nothing at all. Some bodies and some parts of some bodies may be hypersensitive to touch or temperature. People with fibromyalgia, for example, may feel like their bodies are on fire. People with multiple sclerosis may feel cold in their extremities, or that their hands feel the way they'd feel after being in the water too long, but all the time.

This is the part of the body scan where the participants, healthy or chronically ill, take inventory of what they are feeling at that exact moment. Maybe it's calm and peaceful and less or no pain, but maybe it's more pain because you're focusing on your body. Just notice it, whatever it is.

Pay attention to each area of the body. The facilitator asks the participants to notice the feelings in their feet, then their ankles. Continue moving upwards to the calves and the shins, then the knees, thighs, and hamstrings. Continue moving upwards, noticing any feeling in the pelvic region – the buttocks, tailbone, pelvic bone, and genitals. Continue assessing any feeling in your abdomen and stomach, lower back and spine. Then the chest and upper back, including back ribs and shoulder blades. Move on to your hands, palms, wrists, and fingers. Then assess the neck and throat. Then assess the face – eyes, ears, mouth, and nose (try not to sing it, but it's okay if you do), as well as cheeks and forehead. One particular study recommends you finish by assessing the blowhole. If you have no idea what that is on a human, Google will lead you to Urban Dictionary... Let's just say it is NOT necessary to assess the blowhole.

That business aside, the facilitator then brings the participants back to the room, back to the present moment, by asking them to open their eyes. The body scan should not only help you take inventory of how your body feels, but it should also relax you. This is something you'll be able to do on your own, without a facilitator. Again, because we're focusing on mindfulness in the realm of DBT, these exercises will center around group therapy, even if they can be done in individual therapy, or even without a therapist.

- *Mindful Seeing*

An active imagination doesn't come easily to everyone, and mindful seeing may help those who are not blessed/cursed with such. It is similar to observing, but done in a group setting.

Firstly, find space by a window where there are things to be seen outside. Grab a spot fast; the space at the 'staring window' gets filled up quickly.

Notice the things outside, but avoid labeling them. Instead of thinking, *Stop sign* or *Bird*, try to focus on the colors, textures, movements, or patterns. Pay attention to the movement of the leaves and grass. Notice any intricate shapes. Think about this section you see as if you were completely unfamiliar with any of these objects and colors.

Observe without being critical. Be aware without fixating on any one object. If you feel your mind wandering, gently come back by noticing the world again.

In the group discussion, this exercise may spark creativity and inspiration.

- *Mindful Listening*

    Mindful listening is an excellent group activity because people feel validated when they are heard. This activity is used to help the speaker feel heard and the listener to free themselves of inner chatter and actually *listen*.

    The facilitator begins by inviting each participant to think about one thing they are stressed about and one thing they look forward to in the near future.

    After a few moments of thinking, each participant takes their turn sharing their stories to the group.

    The facilitator encourages each client to express how it feels to speak to a group, and how it feels different to speak about stressors or hopes, if at all.

    Participants are encouraged to share their own thoughts, body sensations, and feelings when speaking.

    After everyone has spoken, the facilitator breaks them up into smaller groups to answer questions with each other. The following are some sample questions:

    o How did you feel when it was your turn to speak during the exercise?

    o How did you feel when you listened to the others?

    o Did your mind wander on either occasion?

    o If so, what was the distraction?

- What helped you bring your mind back to the activity?
- Did you find yourself judging anyone who spoke?
- If so, how did your body feel when you were judging?
- How did your body feel right before you spoke?
- How do you feel now?
- What would happen if you practiced mindful listening with everyone?
- Would mindful listening change the way you interact with others?
- If you set the intention to pay attention to every interaction with kindness, curiosity, and openness, how do you think that would feel?

- *The Self-Compassion Pause*

This is a worksheet. It begins by noting the date and asking the participant to notice if the awareness is felt in their heart, body, or thoughts on the current day.

The worksheet provides a short description of the importance of self-compassion for maintaining a higher quality of life. These ideas might include changing the inner dialogue from negative to positive, so you always have a support system, instead of being torn down. Or, by being compassionate towards yourself, you are better able to forgive yourself minor infractions and move on with your day; thus, not creating more infractions by self-loathing.

Next, take a moment to pause both thoughts and actions with a focused awareness that being mindful can help in any area of life.

Then, put a hand over your heart, give yourself a hug, or make physical contact in some way with yourself, and take a few deep breaths.

Next, acknowledge suffering. Do not dwell on it, but acknowledge that it is a part of daily life. Say something like, "This is suffering," and give an example from your own life. Recognize that suffering is a part of being human, and all humans suffer. Say it out loud to be more mindful. Say a phrase that you feel offers self-compassion, such as, "I love and accept myself as I am," or, "I am proud of my accomplishments and working on my flaws." Something that tells your brain you love yourself.

- *Self-Inquiry Meditation*

    This begins the same way as the self-compassion worksheet. Take note of the date and how you are feeling mentally and physically, and what you're thinking about.

    The worksheet offers a short description of self-inquiry and its benefits. It might say something like this: "Checking in with yourself brings you to the present and allows you to know and address any feelings or pain you might have."

    To begin, first take a comfortable seat and allow yourself to settle into your body and mind. Try to let go of thoughts and clear your mind.

    Next, focus your attention on being *you*. What does that feel like? What does that mean? What characteristics make up your core self?

    If you find your mind wandering, bring it back to the exercise by asking, "To whom is this thought occurring?"

    Perform this exercise for as long as you're able. The more you practice, the longer you'll be able to think about your inner self without getting caught up in the hustle and bustle of everyday life.

It brings awareness to yourself in a manner separate from Maslow's Hierarchy of Needs – food, shelter, companionship, etc. Self-inquiry brings awareness to yourself in the manner of "What makes me tick?" or "What makes me unique?" or "What makes me similar to other humans?" or other similar questions.

- *The Five Senses Exercise*

You can practice this exercise in nearly any situation. All that is needed is something you can experience with all five senses.

Start by noticing five things you can see. You can do this without even getting up. Just look around. Pick objects you might not normally notice, like the patterns on a leaf or the cracks in a sidewalk.

Next, notice four things you can feel. These aren't things you need to touch with your fingers. They're things such as the clothing against your skin, the wind against your face, your hands or elbows on the table where you might be sitting, the weight of your body against the chair or seat, etc.

Now, notice three things you can hear. Take a moment to listen and hear things in the background that might get swept up as white noise in everyday life. These things might be the hum of the refrigerator, the air conditioner or fan, the rumble of a distant train, or traffic on another street.

Next, notice two things you can smell, whether pleasant or unpleasant. Notice smells you might normally filter out, like snow (yes, it has a smell) or grass. Maybe it's the restaurant the next block over you've become so accustomed to that you don't notice anymore.

Lastly, notice one thing you can taste. This could be a sip of water, a piece of gum, or a mint. Or just open your mouth to taste the current taste in your mouth or the air, or any bugs that might fly in.

This is a quick exercise to bring you to a mindful state quickly and easily, in whatever surrounding you find yourself in. It brings awareness to the current moment in a short amount of time.

- *The Mini Mindful Exercise*

    This is another exercise to do in a short amount of time. Firstly, step out of "autopilot" to bring awareness to what you are doing, thinking, and sensing right now. Pause and assume a comfortable but dignified posture. Close your eyes. Notice your thoughts, let them arise, and then let them pass. Attune yourself to your current state and who you are, as a person.

    Bring your awareness to your breathing for six deep breaths or one minute, whichever is easier to do without letting your mind wander. Notice the rise and fall of your chest, your stomach pushing in and out. Notice how your lungs expand and contract. Anchor yourself to the present with this awareness by focusing on one single thing: your breathing.

    Next, expand your awareness outward, first to the rest of the body, then to the surrounding environment. When you expand your awareness to your body, notice any sensations you might be feeling, like any numbness or tingling, any burning or aching. Notice any tightness or extreme temperatures, or feeling lightness or heaviness. Remember that your body should not be separated from your mind; it is its vessel as a whole.

    Do further to expand your awareness of your environment. Open your eyes. Notice the colors and shapes in front of you. Notice any sounds or smells. Be present and aware of this particular moment in time.

- *Mindful Walking Down the Street Technique*

    As humans, we can observe our thoughts without reacting to them or needing to fix them. We don't need to hide or solve them. They just are. This awareness creates space for both impulse and planned action, which can help develop coping skills and positive behavioral change.

    The facilitator asks the participant to visualize themselves walking down a familiar street. In this scenario, the client sees someone they know and waves at them but is not greeted back. The other person gives them no recognition in this scenario but just continues walking.

    The facilitator then asks the client, "As you were imagining, did you notice any of your thoughts?" and "As you were imagining, did you notice any of your emotions?"

    The facilitator then asks the client to reflect on the emotions and thoughts and how that affected them. The facilitator asks if this was helpful or not, and if so, how, or why not.

- *The Three-Minute Breathing Space*

    This exercise is designed for people with busy lives, which is most of us. The body scans and meditations require you to keep a clear head, which can be challenging, and only truly obtained by years of practice, if at all.

    This exercise is broken down into three minutes, as the title indicates. The first minute is spent thinking, *How am I doing right now?* with a focus on any thoughts, feelings, or sensations that arise. Label these thoughts or feelings; give them a name.

    The second minute is spent focusing on your breathing. When you feel your mind wandering, bring it back to your breathing.

The last minute is used on focusing on how your breathing affects the rest of the body. Feel the air going all the way down to your lungs. Feel the air as you exhale. Bring your mind back to your breathing when you feel yourself wandering. Focus on the expansion of your lungs, the air coming in your nose and going out of your mouth, or however you breathe.

Your mind will most assuredly wander. This is a difficult exercise to keep the mind from being errant. The idea is not to block thoughts, but to let them come and go, and leave your head clear again. If you actively try *not* to think about something, you *are* thinking about that thing, savvy? Let the thoughts come and go, then disappear again.

These exercises can be used individually or in group settings, by clients or therapists. Mindfulness, like any exercise, takes training to master, and even after you have become a mindfulness Jedi, you will still need to practice daily.

Recognize that mindfulness takes training of the mind, and it will take time to see the benefits of it. It is a new way of thinking, but the key is to persevere. Approach the skill with self-compassion, allow for some leeway and flexibility among techniques, and allow for self-reflection, which may be difficult, but is the most important part of any useful therapy.

Using the How Skills

Nonjudgmentally

As previously stated, each person looks at the world through his or her own lens. Because of this, no person is truly nonjudgmental. We ascribe labels to things, whether consciously or not. Things are "good" or "bad", "moral" or "immoral", "right" or "wrong." We may not even realize we're doing this.

There are some exercises, much like the mindful exercises, that help us practice nonjudgmental mindfulness. Let's discuss a few:

- *Visualize Removing the Lenses of Judgment*

    Imagine you're wearing a thick pair of glasses. You've worn these glasses for so long that you don't even realize you're wearing them. However, they are *your* lenses, through which you view the world. They are layered with *your* experiences, *your* thoughts and opinions, and even the thoughts and opinions of others, simply because they are in *your* sphere of influence.

    Imagine taking these glasses off. In the past, you have put other people's glasses on over these. You have, in the past, even taken off your glasses momentarily to wear another pair.

    But for this exercise, you're just taking your glasses off. You're not putting on someone else's. You're just taking yours off. It feels naked, doesn't it?

    Without your skewed view of yourself, the world, and others, how does everything look now? Try describing yourself in this manner, as objectively as possible.

    In this exercise, try not to use words that connote an opinion, such as handsome. Whereas, attractive is more objective. The word "fat" has negative connotations in society, but if you take away the judgment, it's just a describing word. How do you describe yourself with the glasses on? Might it go something like this: "I'm tall, I'm obese, I have a long nose and blue eyes and red hair. I'm pretty anyway."? How does it sound without the glasses? "I'm tall, I'm overweight, my eyes are blue, my hair is red, I'm average in attractiveness."

    It may sound better or worse without the glasses, depending on how you see yourself.

Describe your best friend with and without the glasses. "She has long hair and crooked teeth. She is the kindest person on the planet, and practically perfect, even if she is an engineer." Now take the glasses off. "She has long brown hair. She has crooked teeth. She smiles easily. She's fit. She is very kind and patient. She is also an engineer."

These examples are fairly similar with and without the glasses. Describe someone you don't like, both with and without the glasses.

"She's nucking futs. She has no sense of reality. She's obsessed with weight and has lost a lot in a short amount of time. She's petty. Her hair is probably either blonde or gray, but it's naturally brown." Now take the glasses off. "She's short, and she's thin – as if she's lost a lot of weight in a short amount of time. Her account of stories does not always tally with others', yet she seems not to realize this. She usually dyes her hair blonde."

The account varies the most with someone you don't like. For many people, the account will vary the most with themselves. Few people see themselves objectively.

- *Mindfully Notice – Really See – Yourself, Others, the World*

    Take a step back, either physically or figuratively, blink a few times, and look at the world around you in a new light, unencumbered by harsh judgments. Allow heavy judgments to fade away into the background until they are gone, and you are viewing yourself, others, and the world without any judgment at all.

    Really ponder the dance of the universe, the stars, God, Buddha, whatever, that led you to be *here*, in this exact spot, at this exact time, with these exact people. Your life literally has been building up to *this* moment.

Allow yourself to realize the intricate dance of all energy, and that *everyone* has lived a life as unique and varied as your own. You may not find your own life very interesting, but someone else will.

Replace judgment, either conscious or not, with compassion. Every single person has had hopes, dreams, fears, love, doubts, failures, regrets, successes, however small or large. Every single person has had privileges others have not, as well as struggles others have not.

Every single person has also been broken at least once, or at the very least been cracked. We build and tear down walls to protect our emotions. We have our false selves and our authentic selves.

Mindfully notice, without judgment, with whom you are your false self, and with whom you are your authentic self.

Try to see through your own walls, through others' walls, or at least understand why they exist. Do so with compassion instead of judgment. Recognize and embrace the common humanity flowing in the blood of all those who are human. Allow the walls and barriers to break down and melt away.

- Ask the Wise Mind, "What is it that I most deeply want *in my life?*"

The Wise Mind, if you recall, is the balance between emotion and reason. It's the perfect Spock of human and Vulcan.

The Wise Mind often represents itself as intuition, a small voice within, or a gut feeling. Don't listen to your heart. It's an idiot. Really don't listen to your libido. It's even dumber. However, your gut is usually a good guide. After you give it pizza.

Wise Mind encompasses both reason and emotion, enabling you to make the most effective choices. If you are truly mindful, an effective decision in the present tense leads to effective consequences in the future. Thinking with the wise mind, while on the surface, seems to be employing the motto, "Hakuna Matata," is in fact, a much deeper decision making skill set.

The decisions made with the wise mind, in the mindful present tense, lead to correct decisions and fallouts from this decision later. Properly take care of the present, and it will take care of the future.

Ask your wise mind, "What is it that I most deeply want in life?" Do not try to force an answer. Instead, try to practice mindfulness. Let answers come and go as they please. After a few moments, you will perhaps notice a pattern.

Maybe you most deeply want to be loved or *to* love. Perhaps you most deeply want a sense of belonging or a feeling of acceptance. Maybe you want a sense of accomplishment, or you seek external validation from specific people.

Whatever answers come to you, choose to practice mindfulness. Direct an attitude of openness, curiosity, and acceptance towards your deepest needs and desires.

- *Mindfulness and Freedom from Suffering*

    Another way to obtain nonjudgmental mindfulness is to subscribe to mindfulness and freedom from suffering. One of the many benefits of practicing mindfulness is learning to release judgment.

    In many instances, people equate judgment with safety. It is a coping mechanism used to avoid getting too close to people, used to tell ourselves that "this type" of person will hurt us. As they say, stereotypes are timesavers, right? However, this is a false sense of security that you can shed at any time.

    By doing so, we allow more openness, and yes, vulnerability into our lives. But we also allow more joy, and thus, less suffering.

- *Harsh Judgments Inflict Unnecessary Suffering*

   Freedom from judgment is attainable, but like all things, is temporary. It must be practiced daily to truly achieve it, if only temporarily. Freedom from judgment by no means approving of something that goes against your core values. It simply means accepting the person as they are.

   Freedom from judgment does not mean, "I love you *anyway.*" The *anyway* is a qualifying term that implies inherent judgment. Freedom from judgment means, "I love you. I see your flaws, and I recognize it's not my place to try to 'fix' them. I accept and love you exactly as you are."

   This does not mean it is not necessary to set boundaries with people. It absolutely is. You can accept someone and love them just as they are while still setting firm boundaries in the relationship.

   Being free of judgment against yourself does not mean you don't work on your flaws. It also doesn't mean, "I love me *anyway.*" It means, "I love me. I'm aware of my flaws, and I'm working to correct them. I'm not aiming for perfection, and I know it's not even possible. I'm aiming for better than yesterday, and even when I backslide, I still love me."

   When you release judgment against yourself and others, you make room for love and acceptance. When you get rid of the judgment, you also release the accompanying fear, anxiety, and doubt.

   Nonjudgmental mindfulness gives you the power to change what is in your control. However, it is difficult to discern what *is* in your control. Nonjudgmental mindfulness enables greater awareness, open-mindedness, and curiosity.

   What happens around you and to you is rarely, if ever, in your control. However, your response, reaction or lack of reaction, and the meaning you ascribe to events *is* within your control.

Human beings are storytellers by nature. When the facts we have don't tell the whole story, we fill in the blanks, either consciously or unconsciously. These "blanks", even at a level below the conscious, *are* within our control because there comes a point in every story that the blanks are at a conscious level. Thus, the *meaning* we ascribe to events *is* within our control.

Human beings are also creatures of habit. We fall into a routine, and whether that pattern is healthy for us or not, we don't often question it until the pain of remaining stagnant outweighs the pain of change.

Look back on your life and your interaction with others. If you are prone to harsh judgment, how has this affected your life? Your relationships? Negatively or positively?

Being nonjudgmental has its pros and cons. However, simply *being* nonjudgmental is not the same as nonjudgmental mindfulness.

No one is *truly* nonjudgmental. Even moments of being, or even seeming, nonjudgmental require practice. However, nonjudgmental mindfulness requires *immense* practice.

Firstly, one must practice being nonjudgmental. This requires some self-reflection and having conversations with yourself that may be difficult. For example, the way you perceive others, does it bring you closer to them or cause a rift? The way you perceive yourself, does it allow for increased authentic self-knowledge? Who do you think you are? Who do others think you are? There will always be a divide, especially depending on the others in question. But is this divide more of a crack or a chasm? Does your mindset allow you to take healthy risks and reach for your value-based dreams?

If you discover that your mindset is more judgmental than you'd like and that it hinders you in some way – from building lasting relationships or pursuing healthy goals – pause for a moment. Step back. Try releasing all judgment. Allow yourself to feel safe in this new sphere of non-judgment.

Nonjudgmental mindfulness is being nonjudgmental in the moment. Practice nonjudgmental mindfulness in some small way every day. For example, if you notice yourself actively engaging with a judgmental thought, allow the thought to linger for a moment, then ask yourself if that line of thinking is productive. This increases mindful awareness and productivity.

If judgment equates to safety, try practicing compassion towards yourself, wherein you still feel safe, but more equanimous. Judgment may feel like your safety zone, but it's never too late to create a new safe space.

One-Mindfully

The idea of one-mindfully incorporates doing only one thing. As humans, we have become so adept at multitasking that we often don't even realize we are doing it.

To be one-mindful, you must start with doing only *one* thing. If you are eating, eat. Don't eat and watch TV. If you are listening to a friend, listen to your friend without bringing out your phone. If you are working, just work; don't worry about what might be going on at home.

The one-mindful practice helps you give your full attention to the task at hand. It helps you do your best job when your mind is not fragmented and distracted.

- *The Orange Exercise*

    Any fruit with a peel will work, but for now, we'll use an orange.

Put the orange on a dish in front of you. Look at it closely. Take your time. Think about where it came from, the tree where it grew, the orchard that housed the tree, the state it may have come from. Think about the other oranges in the grove, the sun, the soil. Think about this particular orange being picked for produce from the tree.

Observe its color and shape. Is it exactly round, exactly orange? Do you notice any markings or dents? What else do you see about this orange? Take your time.

Now begin to peel the orange. Notice that mist may arise from it. Smell the orange. Pull the white part from the peel. Does it feel oilier? Does it smell more bitter?

Pull a section of orange apart from the rest. Notice the texture and smell. Peel the white part from off of the part that holds it together. Is it easy or hard to peel? Are you still struggling with the peel? Do you have to peel the entire orange before you can get a section big enough to eat?

Smell it. Observe it. Does it smell sweet? Does it have seeds? You are in no rush. If your mind wanders to Hans Moleman teaching an orange eating class from *The Simpsons* (it will now. You're welcome), bring your mind back to the orange in front of you. Is your mouth watering? Are you getting juice on your hands? Are you resisting the urge to put it in your mouth like a giant, fake smile? It's a little harder to do that when it's peeled instead of cut, but it's probably still possible. If you struggle with ADHD, bring your mind back to the orange in front of you. Resist the urge to quote *The Simpsons* or smile like an ape. Or do those things, then bring your mind back.

Now bite into the orange. Do you feel the juice dribbling down your chin? Taste the orange. Savor it. Allow the juice to penetrate your entire mouth. How does it taste? Was it perfectly ripe? Not ripe enough? Too ripe? After you swallow this bite, think about how you feel.

Now finish peeling and eating the orange. Can you do it without making a mess? That's okay if not. Savor the taste, the smell, the feel, the sight, and even the sounds of your chewing. Savor the entire experience. Let the orange linger for a bit in your mouth.

You are in no hurry. Is there juice on the dish? The table? Your clothes? Your face? Your hands? Finish eating the orange. Use a napkin to wipe down everything that is messy. Is the napkin now orange? Is it sticky? Are your hands sticky? Did the napkin clean you sufficiently?

For the last few moments, you have just mindfully eaten an orange. Did it taste different than other oranges you've eaten, without thinking about it? How did it feel to be totally present for a few moments during such a pedestrian activity as eating?

Take a few activities during this next week and practice one-mindfulness during regular day-to-day pursuits. Instead of planning out your day in the shower, practice one-mindfulness. Or practice it while walking the dog or listening to a friend or spouse or child. Report back to the group on how being one-mindful during mundane chores changed that task for you that day.

Effectively

Often, we get so caught up in being "right", that we are not always effective. If another driver cuts you off, for example, you legally have the right of way. But is it effective to stay in your lane or keep your speed? It might cause an accident. So, to avoid an accident, you accept the most effective choice and let him in.

In interpersonal relationships, the need to be "right" is even more ubiquitous. Perhaps you are absolutely right about an incident, and the other person is wrong. Is it effective to continue having the circular conversation where nothing is solved? No. It's more effective to let it go and not let your feathers get ruffled when they bring it up. In fact, by having *no* reaction, the other person may lose interest in trying to get a rise out of you.

Many people impose their beliefs, cultures, religion, etc., on others. This behavior is almost always unwelcome.

Is it effective to impose your beliefs right back? Almost always, the answer is no. Actually, always, but again, we're avoiding sweeping generalizations. However, it is effective to set boundaries and tell the person you don't like that. And when they inevitably ignore you, it is more effective to end communication when they do that than to tell them again.

Think about a situation where vengeance, righteous anger, or fear is keeping you from being effective. Would a simple apology mend a relationship? Even if you're right?

That doesn't mean they're allowed to treat you poorly; it just means that you recognize you've treated them poorly, or that it would end tension.

Are you so intent on "getting someone back" that your vision has been clouded as to making effective decisions?

Are you afraid of presenting an idea at work because people might not like it? They also might. It might also be the most effective route possible. It might also start a discussion that *would lead* to the most effective route possible.

Effective mindfulness is coupled with radical acceptance. If, as an extreme example, you suddenly stop walking at 35, and are forced to live in skilled nursing homes, assisted livings, and independent retirement communities, it's more effective to "radically accept" this monumental change than to deny it.

It's more effective to radically accept that your best friend is the polar opposite of you, maybe even the antithesis, on the political scale, than to try to convince her otherwise. People do change their minds, even from one extreme to another, but it is not done by "preaching" your views or guilting them into it. It is done by them living in the opposite camp, as it were, for years or decades and reaching their own conclusion based on evidence.

Chapter Four: Distress Tolerance

Using Crisis Survival: Distraction with Wise Mind

To ease your mind from distress, try following the acronym A.C.C.E.P.T.S.

A – *Activities*

Distract yourself from your distress.

A great distraction for some people with a temporary or semi-permanent crappy personal life is working.

Hobbies are another great way of mindfully distracting yourself. Put all your energy into gardening or painting or fixing old cars.

If you have no hobbies, it's never too late to start. Maybe you've inadvertently collected coins over the years, and now you make a hobby of rolling them. Maybe your hobby is solving puzzles or astrology. It doesn't even have to be something you're good at – just something you enjoy.

C – *Contributing*

Another way to distract yourself is to contribute. Contribute to society or your church or family or friend group. Contribute to the community or a cause that means something to you.

Contributing money, while appreciated, would not distract you enough from your distressing situation or stressor.

Volunteer to teach basketball to inner-city youth. Volunteer at a hospital to watch the kids while the parents talk to the doctors. Ask to babysit your friend's children for a night. Offer to do it for free.

Offer to clean your friend's home while they go out.

Visit a nursing home with your pet and allow the residents to pet it. If it is an exotic pet, like a snake, teach the residents about snakes. Sing the residents a song – just don't opt for "Don't Fear the Reaper"!

Buy flowers for a friend or even a stranger. Male or female. Men like little surprises that smell nice too.

Pick up trash from a public park or highway.

Bring coffee and donuts to a first responder team, like firefighters or police officers.

Send your parents a thank you letter, even if you're not on the best of terms. If they're no longer with us, visit their grave or urn and put flowers on a stranger's plot.

Pay for a stranger's groceries.

Talk to a disabled person like they're a normal human being. That may not sound like much, but it's huge. Everyone knows the "fake voice" or the condescending voice people suddenly assume towards someone after they become disabled.

Write down the times this week when you've contributed to the world outside of yourself. How did that make you feel? Was your behavior in line with your normal behavior? Did you notice you were doing it?

Make a goal this week to go out of your way to contribute in some manner without expecting any reciprocity. This takes you out of your own head and puts your attention on someone else. Write down what you did and how it made you feel, and be prepared to share it in the group.

C – Comparison

You can also distract yourself from your pain and distress by comparison. Some people find it helpful to compare themselves to others. Everyone is at a different spot on their journey to recovery. Everyone has different pasts and backgrounds. As there is no way to know what's going on in someone else's head, it's impossible to judge accurately, and ineffective to even try.

Instead, try comparing yourself to where you were a year ago, a month ago, when the traumatic events in your life began. Compare yourself to where you are now as to where you want to be. You may want to visualize the required steps to get there if that works for you.

Perhaps comparing yourself to fictional characters will also be beneficial to help you distract yourself and help you on your journey. Do whatever works for you.

What do you think about comparisons? Do you find them helpful or do you think they hinder your progression?

E – Emotions

It may also be helpful to distract yourself from your personal distress by invoking the opposite, or at least neutral, emotions from what you are feeling. If you are feeling depressed or empty, try watching a comedy or reading a funny story. Or, if you are feeling empty or melancholy, you may want to watch a drama or read a sappy story – something that brings forth a better emotion. If you are feeling apathetic, which is the lack of emotions, an action movie that makes you think, like *Fight Club* or *Momento,* might suit you better.

Watch a scary movie, listen to silly music, literally dance in the rain – do something that shakes your feelings loose. When you change your emotion, you change where you are in your journey of recovery. You change your mental state of mind and put yourself in a different place emotionally.

Make a mindful decision to change your emotion this week. Write down how you felt, what you did to change your emotion, what you were hoping for, and if you got the desired outcome. Be prepared to share your experiences in the group.

P – Pushing Away

Another coping mechanism to distress is pushing it away. Imagine you're on a castle turret. Imagine throwing your distress off the top. Or imagine you've built a wall between yourself and the problem. Imagine yourself pushing the wall further and further away from you. Imagine putting your distress in a locked box in the closet.

All of these scenarios are temporary. They all allow you to come back to your problem when you are better able to cope with it mentally. These techniques allow you to process the pain. It's still there, it hasn't gone anywhere, but you're able to function and live life without thinking about it.

And then, live your life. Go to work or school. Take care of kids or pets. Go out with friends, watch movies, read books, do the activities you would normally do. When you find your problems creeping back into your brain, imagine throwing them off the turret, or storing them in the box, or pushing them and the wall away from you.

Many times, when we push pain or problems away for a while, the solution seems to have been working itself out in our brains or the pain seems to lessen.

Make a goal of pushing away a particular problem for a few hours or even days. Make a goal of not even talking about it. Write down what you did to push it away and how it made you feel in its absence. Write down if the problem seemed to solve itself or at least become more manageable by the time you came back to it. Be prepared to share it with the group.

T – Thoughts

Distract yourself with other thoughts. Some examples are counting to a hundred, or counting the stars, or counting the tiles in the ceiling. Counting is a good rhythmic activity that takes your mind off your pain, either physical or emotional.

Some people choose to watch a movie or read a book or write poetry to distract themselves from the pain. Some people choose Sudoku or crossword puzzles, jigsaw puzzles or logic puzzles. Try to keep your brain engaged, so it's less likely to wander. Writing may work, or it may make you delve deeper into the pain. Writing it out may help to extract it, to *feel* it less. Thinking of something else is a good distraction when you're in a hurry, in an emergency situation, or in unfamiliar territory. Choose whatever distracting thoughts work best for you.

Think of other ways to distract yourself with thoughts. Make a concerted effort to pull your mind away from your problems this week. Much like pushing away, you may discover that your problems have worked themselves out or seem less astronomical when you return to them.

Write down what thoughts you chose to use to use to keep yourself from thinking about your problems. Write down what you did when your mind began to wander. Write down how you felt both before and after this exercise, and be prepared to discuss these ideas in a group.

S – Sensations

Distract yourself with extreme sensations. A very hot or cold shower is an extreme sensation. If you have access to a hot tub or snow, those will work better. If you have access to both, go from extreme hot to extreme cold very quickly. This distracts you from your pain, as well as amps up the circulation in your body.

Put a rubber band on your wrist and snap it, listen to loud music, watch strobe lights (unless you're epileptic or autistic. Then don't), hold ice on the back of your neck (but do not put salt under it first), hold ice in your hand, touch, very briefly, your steering wheel on a hot day.

Any strong physical sensation can distract you from your pain by jogging loose your connection to your pain, or by adding more to it. Que sera sera. After you've done one of the sensation activities, you may want to do any of the ACCEPT activities again.

Regulate your emotions by utilizing any of these activities, by taking a deep breath and counting to ten, or by saying the alphabet backward before you speak.

When you're angry, and you want to roar, take a deep breath and count to four.

Using Self-Soothe with the Five Senses

Self-soothing is, as the title indicates, something we can do ourselves. We can bring some amount of comfort to our lives. For many people with borderline personality disorder, PTSD, substance abuse, and depression, the main mental illnesses DBT is used for, they have been caregivers for much of their lives, so the idea of caring for themselves may seem foreign to them.

Many people not only don't realize they can and should take care of themselves but don't know where to begin, after crossing that first hurdle. Many people who have a hard time with self- soothing feel like they don't deserve to be happy, or guilty for doing something for themselves.

Many people feel they don't *deserve* to put themselves first in this manner, or they don't *deserve* these comforts. The reality is that everyone deserves to take some time for themselves, to fill their own cup, as it were, so they're not depleted when trying to fill others'.

Again, this is an area that takes practice before it becomes comfortable. Learning a therapeutic skill, unlike learning a cognitive skill, is not a linear process. It may be easy and pleasurable for a time, but then you may feel guilty again. That's the human side of therapy. Everything is perfect until we add humans to the mix.

This next section gives ideas on how to self-soothe by using each of the five senses.

Taste

Try a new dish or a favorite comfort food. Take small bites, savoring each one. Go to a potluck, tasting and savoring a sample at every table. Tell yourself you're Katniss Everdeen in *Mockingjay*.

Drink some hot tea or cocoa, allowing it to sit in your mouth a moment, savoring it. Cook your favorite dish, sampling it as you go.

Be mindful and in the present for each taste. Describe it to yourself to keep your mind on the food.

Smell

Go to a bakery ridiculously early in the morning and smell the delicious aroma of freshly baked bread and pastries. Smell breakfast being cooked from your own home or a nearby restaurant. We do NOT suggest breaking into anyone's home just to smell things, although the inside of a psych ward might have unique smells. Knock yourself out.

Take a walk in nature. Smell the rain or the flowers. Smell the grass or the scent of autumn. It has a unique smell. Smell campfires or barbecues. Breathe in these intoxicating aromas.

Light a scented candle, or choose a particularly delightful wax melt. Notice all the smells around you, and not all of them pleasant. Smell is connected to the part of the brain that houses memories. A certain smell may take you back in time. Bake some cookies. Fill your home with the rich, satisfying aroma of freshly baked goodies.

Try to remain present and focused on the current smell. Be mindful of your surroundings. Describe the smell to yourself as if you'd never smelled it before to stay focused on the present.

See or Vision

Go to a museum. Watch a travel documentary on mute. Walk around town. Notice things you haven't before, like the interplay of light and shadows or the patterns in leaves or grass. Look at an art book.

Go away from the light pollution of the city and find some remote place in the mountains. Notice the stars or look down on the city lights from that angle. Light a candle and watch the mesmerizing flame dance.

Be present and mindful in these activities. Allow your head to clear. Allow yourself to become somewhat hypnotized by the beautiful sights.

Hear

Listen to the sounds of nature, the call of birds back and forth, running water. Listen to crickets and cicadas. Allow yourself to be soothed, rather than annoyed, by the sounds of a busy city. Listen for a rhythmic pattern, which can be found in all things, if you have enough patience.

Get away from the city if that suits you. Listen to the quiet sounds of the night, and realize the night is not so quiet after all. Listen to a cat purr or a baby laugh.

Allow yourself to really be *in* the moment. Discern one sound from the next. What usually sounds like a cacophony, allow it to be broken down and to soothe you instead.

Touch

Take a bubble bath, pet your dog or cat, play with your children in the sandbox. Allow yourself to feel like a child again, feeling the wonder and excitement of each new feel. Put your hands against the outside of a bottle of water right from the fridge or against the outside of a warm oven (where it's still safe to do so).

Put on silk or cotton pajamas, and allow the clothing to breathe. Get a massage, if you can afford it. If you can't, massage your own neck and shoulders.

Allow yourself to really *feel* whatever it is you're touching. Be present and *at* the moment.

Sensory Wrap Up

Feeling guilty about taking care of yourself causes more harm than good. Guilt does not often serve an actual purpose in our daily lives. It will take practice and patience to get over any feelings of guilt you may have.

You may not have as much time as you'd like to practice these activities. Choose ones you do have time for. Write down how you felt before and after – if you were able to stay in the moment – and what you were thinking about if not. Be prepared to discuss it with the group.

You may want to choose one activity per sense over the coming week or one sense and all activities. Do not limit yourself to the suggested activities. If you can think of things that engage a particular sense which is not listed, do them. As you overcome feelings of guilt or thoughts that you don't deserve to be happy, you will be filled with more feelings of joy and peace, and you will be better able to overcome difficult situations in the future, without the excess baggage of guilt weighing you down.

Chapter Five: Using I.M.P.R.O.V.E. the Moment

This next set of skills is best suited for instances when you can't change the setting or situation, don't have much time, and need to change how you feel about the situation.

These skills are used to reduce stress and anxiety, if even for a short amount of time. They can be repeated as often as necessary and are designed to help you feel better. If you can't change your situation or your struggles, you *can* change how you feel about them. Changing something as intricately woven as our feelings, which in many cases have accompanied a specific range of situations for our whole lives, will take time and patience. Be easy on yourself. There are probably enough people in your world ready to tear you down. Don't join them. Step back, take a deep breath, and remind yourself you're doing the best you can.

I – Imagery

Imagine a safe space in your mind – your sanctuary. Maybe it's your home, a friend's cabin, the mountains, the beach, a particular person or animal.

To start, imagine this place when you're not under duress. Maybe go outside or to a library or museum, or someplace peaceful. Maybe physically go *to* this place when you're not under duress.

Notice all the intricate details you may have missed in the past. Notice how you feel. Be able to bring up this place in your mind's eye at the drop of a hat.

When you find yourself in an unpleasant situation, escape to this place in your mind. Breathe. When you come back to the present, you may still be at the board meeting where your colleagues think everything is your fault. But you'll hopefully be at a place of peace now, where you can respond with kindness and logic instead of anger.

Further, imagine *how* you're going to handle conflict when it comes up. If you've walked yourself through the scenario beforehand, you're more likely to keep your cool. Tell yourself you've done this before, that you can handle it, and that you can do a good job, resolving the matter as quickly, effectively, and peacefully as possible.

Practice bringing up this image when you're not under duress for at least a few minutes each day. Write down how you felt before and after this practice. Practice walking yourself through a conflict when you're not in the moment of chaos. Write down what the conflict was and how you resolved it in your mind. Other people are not likely to follow the "script" in your head, so be sure to plan conflict resolution with people who don't really seem to want a resolution. In many instances, this may involve just walking away for a time. Or, if it's your boss, just smiling and nodding, then doing things your own way anyway – being a surface level "yes man" or woman. "Sure thing, boss." Then ignore his ass-backward approach of doing the project, and do it correctly – how you were doing it anyway.

Write down how you handled conflict resolution in your mind and what opportunities you had over the week to use it in real life. Did imagining the conflict resolution help? How so? Or, if not, why not? Be prepared to share with the group.

M – Meaning

Try to ascribe meaning to your pain or trials. Not everything happens for a reason. However, if you can find a meaning or a silver lining in everything, it will help you better able to come to terms with it.

An anecdote Viktor Frankl uses in *Man's Search for Meaning* is when asked by a fellow Holocaust survivor why his wife had to die, Frankl had asked him how his wife would feel if she were still living and he was not. The man then ascribes the meaning of her death to him having to suffer *instead* of her. His situation hasn't changed; his wife is still dead. But it is now easier for the man to continue living without her, remembering that he'd rather take on her pain.

Ascribing meaning to an event doesn't change the event. It doesn't take the pain away. It doesn't mean this event *had* to happen in order for you to be happy or live a full life. Perhaps its only purpose was for you to learn or do something specific, at that time.

Whatever your situation is, the loss of a child, a house fire, a traumatic brain injury, an event or series of events that caused PTSD, finding meaning won't change the reality of the situation. However, it will make the situation easier to deal with on a day-to-day basis.

If you had a bad day at work, and the next day it's over, and life is fine again, it may not be necessary to ascribe meaning to a menial day, but it wouldn't hurt either. It might be good practice to do so, so that when you think about life-altering events, it may be easier to ascribe meaning.

P – Prayer

One does not have to subscribe to a religion to utilize the power of prayer. You can pray to any higher being you might believe in, any theocratic being you might believe in, or simply to the universe.

If you don't believe in any higher beings, including the universe, believe in yourself. You know you're going to get through whatever daunting task is ahead of you because your survival rate of bad days is, thus far, 100%. Those are pretty good odds. So pray to your future self. Ask your future self how you got through this, whom you asked for help.

The conversations between your present self and future self should take place in your head or when you're completely alone for several reasons. If others are around, you'll either earn yourself a trip to the psych ward or accidentally make friends with someone who should probably be there.

Further, if you actually *see* your future self, there's a good chance you broke the space-time continuum, and if that's the case, please, please, please, take the almanac back from Biff. He's destroying the world at an alarming rate.

Pray to whomever, in whatever capacity, works for you. Allow others to pray for you. More positive energy in the world with your name on it is never a bad thing. You may have a different religion from your friends and family or none at all, but if they think they're helping, let them. Even if they actually practice witchcraft, what are the odds they're going to be able to hurt you? Or want to, if they can? Let people pray for you. Pray yourself. Or meditate. Meditation is getting in touch with your spiritual side. You don't need to believe in any higher power to do that.

R – Relaxation

Relax. Take a hot bath or a cold shower or whatever relaxes you. Lie in the grass, with the warm sun on your back, read a book on your back patio, smoke a doobie on your porch (where it's legal – if you have a prescription for it), walk your dog, and meditate.

Do whatever activity helps you relax. Talk to your loved ones who have passed on in your mind. Call a friend, watch a movie, drink a box – whoops glass – of wine, eat some chocolate, have sex, paint, draw, color. Use those adult coloring books for relieving anxiety and tension. No, not *that* kind of adult. The details are just so intricately designed that a child couldn't stay in the lines. Coloring has been proven effective in reducing stress.

Take a yoga class (it's actual exercise, so dress accordingly), or a yodeling class.

Take a relaxing walk, breathe deeply for a few minutes, start a conspiracy theory. Get a massage, get your hair done, get a mani-pedi, spend money you don't have on clothes you'll probably only wear once. Go to a bar. Watch a game. Go fishing. Play video games. Clean. Go to work to escape home. Go home to escape work. Go to a gun range. Go out with friends. Turn off your phone and close your blinds. Do whatever relaxes you.

We tend to tense up during stressful situations, and our bodies go into a fight, flight, or freeze mode. Few people realize that *freeze* is a valid reaction, and we don't get to choose our reactions.

Think back on times you were tense or stressed or scared. How did you react? Call up those stressful moments in your mind, then do something that alleviates the stress. Next time you're in a stressful situation, breathing deeply and counting to ten will come much easier. Engaging in relaxing activities calms the psyche.

O – One Thing at a Moment

Try to keep your mind focused on the moment. Thinking about past injustices does nothing to solve the problem at hand. Planning for every possible contingency in the future, while helpful in some capacities, is not helpful during the moment of crisis.

Even during the moment of crisis, it's not like TV, where there's only one problem at a time. In real life, problems don't march in a straight line like ants on a mission. They jumble on top of each other, like ants on a cookie.

Make a concerted effort to separate one problem – one ant – from the pack. The others are still there; they haven't gone away. And problems are all interwoven with each other, like a spider web. You can't separate one strand from the others because they all overlap in the center.

So taking one thing at the moment requires, like everything else, patience and practice. Don't be too hard on yourself. Make an effort to tackle just one issue. If it's easier to start with the hard ones, do so. If it's easier to start with the easy ones, do so. Either way, you'll find as you continue tackling one issue after another, one issue takes care of another.

Find one thing to devote your entire self to. Having a one-track mind helps emotions and tasks not feel so overwhelming.

V – Vacation

Ideally, we'd be able to vacation whenever we wanted. However, even in the make-believe world of impromptu vacations, we still have to come back to the real world, where our stressors seemed to have doubled in our absence.

But in our world in our heads, we can take a vacation in our mind. Such play is vital to a child's learning. Why do we stop when we become adults? Now, if we have imaginary friends or think the floor is lava, we're labeled schizophrenic.

So all we can do to keep this sense of childlike wonder and imagination alive is to vacation in our minds. Go someplace you've been before in real life. Or go someplace you've only read about.

But go on a mental vacation for a few minutes. Feel the sun on your face, the sand between your toes.

Order a delectable meal. Tip the server hundreds of dollars. This is all imaginary. Take an evening stroll under the stars. Go on a hike in the mountains.

Keep smiling and nodding, and none's the wiser that you're not really present. And when you do "return", you'll be in a better mindset and better able to handle your daily stressors again.

E – *Encouragement*

Encouragement doesn't have to be external to be valid. Give yourself encouragement. Repeat encouraging mantras to yourself, out loud when you can, or in your head when you can't say it out loud. "I got this!" or "I can do it!" or "I can make it through this moment. It's only temporary. I can do this."

Saying this often enough actually rewires the brain to believe it. When you say encouraging phrases to yourself over minor inconveniences, they'll be easier to say and to believe over large infractions. You might just amaze yourself at how much you're able to accomplish. Think about what you've done thus far. Imagine how much more you can do as your own best fan club.

I.M.P.R.O.V.E. Skills Wrap-Up

These skills can be used at any time in any place. If you're not currently practicing DBT therapy, these skills are still a fountain of knowledge. If you practice these techniques when you have little to no stress, they'll come easier to you when you need them.

Pros and Cons

Every decision we make every day has both pros and cons. Every decision causes a domino effect of millions of other decisions, large and small. We can't be expected to know how each decision will affect every person in our circle, nor can we be expected to accept responsibility for their actions based on the domino effect of our decisions.

When we are in our wise mind, decision making is easier, more fluid. We still cannot see how our decisions will affect our lives next year, next month, maybe not even tomorrow.

However, a pro and con list helps put us in our wise mind and helps us plot out the possible short-term outcomes of our decisions.

Many people in a state of a crisis have the urge to self-harm. When you're in that state of mind, you won't be thinking about a pro and con list.

To this end, it's imperative, like the IMPROVE skills, that you practice them when there is no crisis so that you'll be better able to recall the skill when there *is* a crisis.

For example, make a pro and con list of something simple, just to get you in the habit.

Taking the dog on a different route

Pros:

- I get to see new things.
- I get to meet new people.
- He might love it.

Cons:

- He might take forever.
- I *have* to meet new people.
- He might hate it (but he's a dog, so probably not).

This list gives us equal pros and cons, with about the same weight to either decision, the list leaning slightly in favor of pro. So, go ahead and take the dog on a different route!

Not all pro/con lists need to be written out, but it's a good habit to get into. If you self-harm in crisis mode, it's a good idea to be in the habit of writing pro/con lists.

Firstly, it will distract you from the immediate urge to self-harm. Secondly, you can differentiate between behaviors that are absolutely horrible for you and behaviors that your body can tolerate. In this manner, you may eventually be able to stop cutting and trade it for lifting weights. Let's make an example pro/con list of two different behaviors.

Cutting

Pros:
- Pain makes me feel alive.
- People might see I need help.
- It feels good for a second.
- The sight of blood calms me.

Cons:
- It hurts.
- People are nosy.
- It might get me sent to a psych ward.
- I don't actually like blood.
- I might go too deep or hit a vein.
- I don't actually want to die; I'm just sick of living.
- It leaves scars.
- People ask about the scars.
- I become a project instead

Overeating

Pros:
- Food tastes good.
- It reminds me I'm alive.
- It can be done socially or alone.
- I can pass it off as a joke.
- No one needs to know I'm not okay.

Cons:
- I might gain weight.
- It gets expensive.
- I might *want* people to know I'm not okay.
- I might get food poisoning.

of a person.
- It might send me to the hospital.
- Covering it up or paying for hospital bills gets expensive.

From these examples, we can clearly see that of the two self-harming behaviors overeating is a much less dangerous one. The chronic cutter knows this too.

However, impulses aren't led by the wise mind. They're led by what Homer Simpson describes as "the impulse zone", which is where he lives. And that's all well and great for him because he's a fictional character.

For us, for real flesh and blood people, our decisions have actual consequences in the real world.

Self-harm behaviors are *all* led by the impulse zone. But if you can refrain from acting on those urges long enough to make a pro and con list of separate behaviors, you'll be able to connect with your wise mind. You may only connect with it briefly, and still carry out a self-harming behavior, but it will be the lesser of two evils.

Eventually, you may be able to resist the urge to self-harm and write pro and con lists for weightlifting or deep cleaning.

Making pros/cons lists in your head and on paper about a single decision, or weighing one decision against another, will be useful in fighting impulse urges and cleaning up after their negative outcomes.

DBT is a useful skill set to have in many areas. The next section discusses *using accepting reality* as a skill set.

Chapter Six: Using Accepting Reality

Willingness

Willingness, in this context, means cultivating a *willing* response to each situation. Willingness requires listening to the wise mind and behaving in an effective way for each situation.

Willingness is listening to your inner self and becoming aware of your connection to the universe. It is, at once, recognizing the awesome power you hold within you as well as recognizing your insignificance in the grand scheme of this universe and others.

We are, at the same time, the center of many worlds – yet also a speck of dust on the beach. It's bewildering to think about.

When you are distressed, before you react, ask yourself: "Will the situation causing me distress *now* matter in five years?"

Often, the answer is no. Sometimes, the answer is yes – but we think it's no. We have no idea what the future holds.

Willfulness

Willfulness is finally having reached the conclusion that *something* must be done, but deciding it's too hard. It's giving up when you're almost there. This subject needs to be touched on because it's easy to give up. It's easy to get kicked down by life. It's easy to stay there. However, it's harder to stay there when you *know* you can get back up. When the pain of stagnation is worse than the pain of change, you'll change.

Turning of the Mind

Turning your mind is the beginning of accepting reality. It's a fork in the road. But not both options are real and valid. One option is reality, and the other option is anything else. Sometimes our brains don't let us process reality in order to protect us. Sometimes we *choose* not to accept reality. And because we all look at the world through our own spheres and lenses, reality can seem to be a many-varied beast. In truth, it is a *memory* that is a many-varied, many-headed beast – but the reality is not skewed towards anyone's favor. It just is.

It is at this point in the fork in the road that we must choose if we are going to accept reality *as it is* or continue to try to manipulate reality to be *as we'd like it.* If we're serious about therapy, we seek out actual reality. We have a little "come to Jesus" meeting with our brains. Or come to whomever.

If we choose to accept the fork in the road that *is* a reality, it's a conscious decision. And we may need to make it several times in the space of a few minutes. Accepting that we will accept reality is the first step. It's like trying to try. However, accepting to accept reality is stronger than trying to try. It's accepting that maybe you haven't always been amazing at determining reality in the past. Self-awareness is huge.

At this point in other therapeutic assignments, you may have given up and turned to the other fork which was denial or comfort, or anything else. Because the reality is often harsh, we want to avoid pain. Pain is a warning that something is wrong and we need to leave the situation.

However, physical pain and psychological pain are as different as night and day. Physical pain is a good thing. It tells us to leave before we are permanently damaged – if we can get away. Psychological pain doesn't usually show up until *after* we have become psychologically damaged, and then seemingly unrelated things are triggers.

When we choose to turn the mind, we make the conscious choice to choose to deal with the pain instead of running back to the safety of denial or comfort. Denial and comfort are great. But if we don't deal with the pain, it keeps coming back until we do. It's worse than annoying relatives and probably caused by a few. Just living requires an amount of pain. You have to be comfortable with a certain level of pain, physically or psychologically or both.

Turning of the mind requires a commitment to deal with the pain until it's down to the level that doesn't impede your life. Only you can make that decision. No pain would be ideal, but that's just not reality.

Radical Acceptance

Earlier we discussed "radical acceptance" in conjunction with mindfulness. "Radical acceptance" is nothing more or less than accepting what life has presented to a reality.

Take this example. A woman is diagnosed with multiple sclerosis and attends support groups. She had to use a walker to get around. She mentions in one group that she's looking to buy a trailer home that already has a wheelchair lift.

Her idea gets shot down immediately.

"If you think you'll end up in a wheelchair, you will. Don't think like that! Just think positive!" a few of the group members say.

Those three words have become the bane of her existence, and she mentally throat punches anyone who says them now.

Thinking she will or won't end up in a wheelchair isn't going to stop the progression of a debilitating disease.

Now, the idea of her being able to afford a home, even a trailer home, being able to take care of herself – that's far superior to what is now her reality: living in a retirement home at 38. But this is the best home she's lived in since she stopped walking at 35.

Thinking you're going to end up in a wheelchair isn't being negative. In the woman's case, it was being realistic. Thinking you can't be a productive member of society from a wheelchair is thinking negative.

So, when bad stuff happens, and it does, you accept it as reality. That doesn't mean you have to like it, and it doesn't mean you have to stay in that situation forever. It means "this is my reality now. What's next?"

If, after too many years, you finally realize you're in an abusive relationship, for example, you say, "This is my reality now. What's next?" And you plan for ways to get out of it. Or you plan for ways for your kids to get out of it. Or you retreat to safe spaces in your head until you can get out of it. But you do *something*.

Radical acceptance is a bit of an oxymoron. It means accepting yourself *just as you are*, but at the same time, *working on yourself to change self-sabotaging behaviors*.

Radical acceptance means letting go of how things "should be" and accepting them as they are. Ironically, radical acceptance is the first step toward real change.

When you let go of an image, of a "should be", you release judgment from that person or idea. When you let go of how you "should be", and accept yourself for who are, and who you are not, only then can you affect change – only after you've released judgment from yourself.

Radical acceptance also means releasing others of judgment. As discussed earlier, every moment you've been alive, and even prior, has been building up to this particular moment in time. It kind of gives you a bewildering scope of existence, huh?

So whatever position you find yourself in now, some of that is your fault, and some it is others', and some of it is to your credit, and some of it is to others'. And some of it belongs to no one; it just *is*. However, none of that matters. Where you are is where you are. Portioning out blame or credit solves nothing. People are much more likely to portion out blame than credit – and much more likely to say they got to where they are with no help from anyone. That isn't true, and it's irrelevant.

Radical acceptance means accepting that you *were* born into some privileges and that people before you *did* pave your way. It's also accepting that not all of the shit in your life *is* your fault and that maybe karma is a load of crock. Maybe not. But either way, *it doesn't matter*.

Because now that you've accepted all of this, and you've released judgment from yourself and others, you say, "I've accepted it. Now what?"

Now what indeed.

Now that you've accepted that good things happen to bad people and bad things happen to good people, and the world just keeps on spinning, you've reached a pivotal point in your life and in your path to healing.

Now what?

Now you're at a crossroads. You can continue living as you have, accepting the reality of any situation, or you can cause some change in your behavior or mindset that will ameliorate the situation.

You've accepted that it *is* a reality – but it doesn't have to *stay in* reality.

Chapter Seven: Emotion Regulation

Using the acronym P.L.E.A.S.E., we'll next discuss emotion regulation through reducing vulnerability.

P & L – Treating Physical Illnesses

Listen to your body when it whispers so that you don't have to hear it scream. We often push ourselves more than we should – maybe more than we can. Have you noticed when you're crazy busy for a few weeks, as soon as you have time to breathe, *that's* when you get sick? It's because you've pushed your body to its limit, and when you took a break, it forced you to recover.

Take your prescribed meds as prescribed. Listen to your doctor. Find one who listens to you. Work together with your body and your doctor. Don't wait until you *have* to see a doctor to go. Go for a yearly checkup.

The Western world is amazing at separating the body from the mind when it's all connected. When you feel well physically, you're less likely to have stress spiral out of control. Take care of your body. Drink your Ovaltine. Take your vitamins. Sleep. Some people can function on six hours of sleep every night. Some people need ten. Listen to your body.

Brush your teeth. Floss. Eat your veggies. No, your mother did not suddenly learn how to infiltrate your apps. Exercise. Not with the goal of losing weight, but if you do, great. Exercise because it feels good. So does eating cheesecake. Do that too. Fat doesn't mean unhealthy, and skinny doesn't mean healthy. To hell with what you're "supposed to" look like, and look like what feels healthy. Back to radical acceptance. There is no "supposed to".

Take care of your body. You're going to be together for quite some time. It's time you became friends with it.

E – Balanced Eating

Eat when you're hungry, not bored. Stop eating when you're full. Yes, there are children starving in Africa, and that's a shame. Try not to take more than you need. Eat breakfast. Eat a healthy lunch instead of vending machine snacks. Eat a light dinner before you unwind. Limit your meat intake. You know all of this. Living it is entirely different from saying it. But again, when you feel physically well, your emotions don't get out of whack so easily.

A – Avoid Mood-Altering Drugs

This really should go without saying, but when you're using mood-altering drugs, not prescribed by your doctor, not in a manner prescribed by your doctor, you're... well, altering your mood. That's going to mess your emotions up. That's kind of a given. However, what may need a reminder is that there comes a point when you *can't* control your emotions when you take drugs. There comes a point when you become addicted as well. Both of these points are scary points. To not be in control of your own emotions is frightening for you and others. Know what your cutoff point of alcohol is as well. When you are inebriated, you're not making the best decisions, and "I was drunk" is a lousy excuse for an excuse. You're an adult now. You know what you're like when you're drunk. You know what your cutoff point is. Avoid going past that point.

S – Balanced Sleep

These all overlap with each other, because taking care of our bodies is such a many-faceted ideal. If you need more sleep than what your work schedule or children allow, find a way to get more sleep. Just downing more caffeine is only a Band-Aid fix and actually does more harm in the long run. Cut back on watching television, or go to work earlier in the morning so you can sleep earlier at night. Or whatever works for you. Find a way to make it work. Stop procrastinating on projects. Listen to your body.

E – Get Exercise

If all you have time for is work, take the stairs instead of the elevator. Take a walk around the building after lunch. If you watch TV every night, swap a few of those nights for swimming or walking around the neighborhood. You really do feel better when you exercise. Build up to twenty minutes a day. When your body is healthy, you're less inclined to be susceptible to an emotional roller coaster.

Using Mastery

Using the mastery skills in this section will help you achieve Wise Mind. When you practice Wise Mind when the seas of life are calm, it will be easier to bring to mind those skills during turbulence.

Doing *something* that makes you feel a little better every day helps relieve stress and inspire confidence. Attaining confidence helps reduce stress in stressful situations as well as everyday situations.

Taking care of yourself helps you to stay grounded so that when crap happens, and it will, you can keep your cool and maintain a consistent level of emotions.

Build Positive Experiences

Building positive experiences is necessary for emotion regulation in that we need a well of positives to draw from when we're running on empty. Many experiences are wonderful at the time, and then we later may not be friends with the people we had the experience with. Do not let that mar the memory. Remember who they were when you made the experience together. There are two important categories in which to build positive experiences: the short term and the long term.

Short Term

The short-term memories include talking to a good friend, taking a walk, noticing the beautiful area, going to the dog park, reading a good book, watching a show or movie you love, dining out, having a picnic, laughing on a break with a coworker. Most of us already do something to create short-term positive experiences daily without thinking about it.

This exercise is asking you to create more short-term positive experiences and do it deliberately. Call up an old friend. Stay off social media after work for a few days. Make a concerted effort to tell ridiculous, silly stories with your kids. Send your nieces and nephews presents from the clearance aisle. Do something that will create positive experiences deliberately.

When you deliberately practice making and noticing positive experiences, you'll begin to make and notice more as part of your daily life. When positivity is a part of your daily life, you feel better emotionally and physically.

Do at least one of these things, or choose something else that makes you happy, every day for a week. Go out of your way to do it for a week. After that, try to make it IN your way. Do something you've never tried before. There are probably a few things you've never thought of trying:

- reading a good book
- writing a good story
- going out for drinks midweek
- going to a movie midweek
- sex
- eating a good meal
- going out for just dessert
- going to a poetry jam
- going to a karaoke bar
- joining in a pub trivia with friends
- learning to make sushi or another exotic dish
- trying a new exotic dish
- jogging
- kickboxing
- swimming
- watching a children's movie in the theater and focusing on the laughter
- stopping on the dog walking route to smell the flowers
- doing something nice for a stranger
- doing something nice for a friend
- playing a carnival game
- getting the expensive, full inside-out car wash
- getting your to-do list completed
- writing a ridiculously easy to do list so you can complete it
- taking pictures with a real camera
- going down a waterslide

- playing board games with friends
- playing interactive games, like "How to Host a Murder"
- going to a movie or a concert in the park
- going to a new hobby class like painting or writing or learning to skate
- organize your bookshelf or closet
- buy a new article of clothing or jewelry or book for yourself
- visit a nursing home to sing or play bingo with the residents
- let your kids teach you their favorite video game
- get a massage
- go to the chiropractor
- go to a play or the opera
- go to a high school play
- go to a college football game
- drive to a different city for dinner with a friend
- go sightseeing
- join Toastmasters
- volunteer at a homeless shelter during the months they really need it: January-October
- carry "homeless packs" in your cars: gallon Ziploc bags with personal hygiene materials, feminine hygiene products, smokes, granola bars, bottles of water, socks, candy bars, stuffed animals, cash, gift cards to McDonald's, etc. Put them with blankets, coats, clothes you would've given away. Drive around the areas where there are homeless people and give these out
- garden
- plan a party

- get your hair done
- talk in a different accent for an evening
- dedicate a song on the radio station to someone
- write in your journal
- spend some time alone without television, radio, or internet; just you and a cup of the beverage of your choice
- go out to lunch with a friend
- play volleyball
- play hide and seek with your coworkers (and try not to go home when their eyes are closed)
- sing in the car
- drive to the mountains
- roast marshmallows
- go to the sauna
- sit in a hot tub
- sit in a cold tub
- make a fort in the elevator at work with a sign that says, *No bosses allowed!*
- silently challenge the driver in the car next to you at a stop light to a dance off in your cars
- do a Chinese fire drill (what's the pc term for that?)
- keep a box of fruit snacks in your desk for anyone having a bad day
- song fight with your spouse
- convince a stranger you think you're a vampire
- call a radio station and tell them a funny story
- do a jigsaw puzzle

- ride a unicycle
- go to a museum or aquarium
- go to a psychic, just for giggles
- get a Reiki session done
- take a stuffed animal for a walk, pretend to cry when anyone points out it's not real
- call a radio station and pretend to be a psychic. Google the DJ while you're talking and tell them all about themselves so they'll believe you
- go to a belly dancing class

Long Term

Long-term positive experiences are more goal oriented, creating a life worth living. What are some goals that you would like to achieve? Write down a few specific goals. Break them down into subcategories.

<u>Money</u>

1. One common goal people have is money oriented. Write down how much you'd like to save each month or put towards your debt. If you put it in a place you'll forget or an IRA (Individual Retirement Account) you can't touch, you're less likely to spend it.

2. Learn how to budget. Keep track of how much you spend versus how much you make. Keep track of all your expenses. See where you can cut back. Itemize your spending as you go – keep it on your phone until you put it into a spreadsheet. When tax time comes, you already know how much you spent on medical supplies or work-related expenses. Use your debit card instead of your credit card. Then you're only spending what you have, and if you don't keep your receipts, everything is on your bank statement anyway.

3. Get out of debt as much as possible. You may always have debt for education, health, and home (go, 'Murica), but you can pay off your credit cards and chip away at the others. Unless you get total and permanent disability, then no more student loans! But if you do it on purpose, it's apparently a fraud.

4. Save as much as possible. Save by packing your own lunch instead of eating out. Put that in a jar. Use those coins when your kid needs shoelaces or something. After a while of paying with change, you forget you ever had any dignity; it's cool.

5. If your job offers a 401(k), take it. Immediately. The 401(k) follows the person, not the job. If your job offers overtime, do it. Pick up shifts. Show up in your uniform and ask who wants to go home. When a couple complains that they don't know where their waitress is, promise to take care of them yourself because she clearly doesn't value her customers. Then pocket that $20 tip and yell at yourself in the mirror. Find little tricks to make your job and your screw ups work FOR you.

Relationships

1. Repair a relationship.

    If you have a relationship in your life that you feel must be repaired in order for you to move on with your life, you may have to take the initiative. You may have to make the first move, offer the first apology. Not a fake "I'm sorry you feel that way" apology, but a sincere "I'm sorry I treated you that way apology." Not even a half-sincere apology – "I'm sorry I treated you that waym but you deserved it and here's why." Let that second half come about if they accept your apology and you can open a discussion.

2. End a relationship.

> Not all relationships can be saved, and not all should be. If you have offered a sincere apology and have been rebuffed, it may be time to cut your losses and move on. It may be sad for both of you, but some relationships, while once were good, over time have become toxic for one or both parties. If this is the case, you might try one last ditch effort, and then you should actually ditch it. If they come back, you'll see how you feel at that time, if it's something you want to renew. Some relationships are better off dead. Reviving those is the true zombie apocalypse.

3. Create new relationships.
    a. The older we get, the harder it is to create new relationships. We have to actually go out of our comfort zones to meet new people. Talk to people at your bowling league. Start a bowling league. Talk to new people at functions you do on the regular, like church or kayaking or suing people. Or even family reunions.
    b. Go to weekly things. Join Toastmasters. You'll migrate towards the same people each week, but how much do you really talk to them? Get to know someone, more than just surface level. Ask probing questions like, "If you invented a superpower, what would it be?" None of this already invented superpower business. That's boring. "You can travel to the past, before a huge disaster, with the ability to warn people, but you might get stoned or burned as a witch, or you can travel twenty seconds into the future every day. Which do you choose?"

4. Work on current relationships.

   a. Work on maintaining the relationships you have. Keep the status quo. Or change it. The status is not quo. Develop deeper bonds with people. Do you really know their hopes and fears, wishes and dreams?
   b. Go out of your way to stay in touch. Most friendships are built on convenience – when it's convenient for both or all parties to talk or hang out. Texting is a great way to let them know you're thinking about them, and they'll respond when they can. It's also a great way to miscommunicate, but that can be done in any medium.

Positive Mindfulness

1. Be mindful of positive experiences.

   Practicing mindfulness while you're doing something you enjoy helps to savor the moments. Stay focused on the positive experience and refocus your mind as often as necessary. This will get you in the habit of mindfulness and focusing on the positive aspects of the day or the moment. The more we focus on something, the more we notice it. That's just how our brains work. That's not to say it is actually more prevalent, but it is certainly more prevalent in our minds, which is where we have to live, so we may as well learn to enjoy the company.

2. Be unmindful of worries.

   Distract yourself from thinking you don't deserve this happiness, or when the positive experience will end or what chores need to be done elsewhere. Distract yourself from thinking about what awaits you at the end of the positive experience, or worrying about how much money you're spending on it. If you're at the circus, for example, instead of thinking, *I don't deserve to be enjoying this*, focus on your surroundings – children laughing, cotton candy, the rides, the clowns. Unless you have a deep fear of clowns. You might not want to focus on them then. Damn you, Stephen King!

3. Practice.

There is a lot of material in this section, and no one expects you to conquer it overnight. You shouldn't either. Like any habit, it needs to be practiced before it becomes an actual habit. And then it still needs to be practiced.

Be Mindful of Positive Emotions

Get in the habit of noticing your emotions and recognizing if they're negative or positive. When they're negative, get in the habit of not dwelling on them. When they're positive, get in the habit of being mindful of the actual emotion. "I'm happy right now. It feels warm. It feels calm." Describe how the emotion feels to yourself, instead of getting caught up in *why* you're happy or peaceful, or what have you.

Using the Opposite to Emotion Action

What actions do you do with negative emotions? They're probably the go-to actions, preprogrammed by your psyche. It takes time, but you can reprogram your psyche by using the opposite actions you normally use. When you're afraid, your brain kicks in to fight, flight, or freeze mode. In some instances, it's still a very vital response mechanism developed for our own safety. In other instances, the response mode has been passed down from our hunter/gatherer ancestors and serves no real purpose today. For example, test anxiety. It's real.

However, a test doesn't present the need for a fight/flight/freeze response that imminent death, beating, rape, a car accident, or a full-grown saber-toothed tiger would pose. However, the reaction is still the same, and we don't get to choose our subconscious reactions.

But we do choose our conscious actions. In the test anxiety example, try giving yourself many practice tests to lose anxiety.

Perhaps your fear is roller coasters. Go more often, with someone you feel safe with, to desensitize you. Try to desensitize yourself to the fear. If your fear is clowns, go to McDonald's more. No need to hang around real clowns. Those freaks will eat you in your sleep.

If your reaction to anger is to yell and throw things, step away from the situation that makes you angry and work on breathing exercises. Unless you're driving. Then just work on breathing exercises.

If a particular person or politician makes you angry, try to find the small amount of truth they may have said in order to gain sympathy or empathy, or at the very least, not hatred. Scratch that. Turn off the television. Work on that with a real person in your life rather than a politician.

If your go-to reaction to sadness is self-isolation, take the opposite approach. Get out in the community and volunteer. Go out with your friends. Go to an ice cream store by yourself, just to get out of the house. And have some ice cream.

If you're feeling shameful, the first question to ask yourself is, "Why am I feeling like this?" Is it because you did something you're ashamed of? Admit it to yourself and your haters, then move on. The longer you deny it, the longer it draws out the feeling and adds further negative emotions to it, like anger. If you've done nothing wrong, but are being dragged through the mud for pointing out someone else did, welcome to the patriarchy. Even males can be oppressed by it. Just hold your head high and live your life. People will soon see who you really are. And those who don't see it often filter out. Let them.

Guilt works in many ways the same as shame. If you need to offer a sincere apology, do so. Your refusal to do so, whether it's accepted or not, whether they've offered one or not, whether they actually deserved whatever action you need to apologize for or not – that's all irrelevant. Your refusal to do so only draws the time out longer and drives the wedge in further.

The opposite reaction works best when the emotion does not fit the scenario. If you should be angry at something, it's still best to breathe deeply and assess the situation calmly. However, the other person is allowed to know you're angry. If your anger motivates you toward positive change, so much the better.

Chapter Eight: Interpersonal Effectiveness

Using Objectiveness Effectiveness (D.E.A.R. M.A.N.)

D – Describe

Describe the event using facts only. Do not use emotions. Let it speak like a police report if you do use emotions. "Patient seemed upset." It works better to sound like a police report if you talk in the third person. However, don't take this habit in the real world. That's just confusing. Don't make a request or "dry beg". Dry begging is saying obnoxiously passive-aggressive things like, "I really need thirty bucks," or, "Wow, that cake looks good. I wish I had some." The best response to dry beggars is: "Yep. You do." Or it could be, "Yep. It is." If they really want it, they'll get around to asking like an adult. It might go like this – say you're from a religious family, and your teenager decides not to go to church. You might reply, "I've noticed you don't like church. Let's discuss the options of staying home."

This is important so that the other party understands clearly what the situation is before you ask anything, entreat, or make an executive decision.

E – Express

Express yourself with "I feel" or other "I" statements. These types of statements help the speaker take accountability and prevent the listener from immediately going into defense mode. Let's go back to the teenager staying home from the church example. Now, you might say something like, "I feel like you should believe what I believe, but I know that you're your own person, separate from me, and I can't force my beliefs on you. I would like you to come to church with us because my worry is you won't be productive at home."

This is important so that the other party understands where you're coming from when you express how you feel about the situation you've just described.

A – Assert

Assert your position by either directly asking for what you need or stating your position clearly. Don't beat around the bush, don't use euphemisms, and don't hesitate to the point of losing the other party's interest. To continue with the example, let's assert our decision for our hypothetical teenager. "I understand that you don't want to come to church with us, and you are old enough to stay home alone. So, if you choose to stay home instead of attending church, you will prepare dinner and set the table and have everything prepared for us to be able to eat when we return, and you will make enough in case we invite people over unexpectedly. If you are unable to complete this chore, and thus, be productive for the whole family while we are at church, you will come back with us, even if you don't believe it."

This is important because ambiguity creates miscommunication in relationships, and that is the biggest source of contention. Be unambiguous. Set the boundaries now. If you're making a request, it must also be unambiguous, maybe even a little lawyerly.

For example, you might say, "Can I please borrow your car from Sunday to Tuesday? I'll return it by 7:00 pm with a full tank of gas and a wash."

The other party might have other caveats. Such as, "Yeah, but it overheats, so don't go over 55 mph, or over 55 miles away. And my tags are expired, so avoid cops. Or renew it for me."

In which case, you might say, "You know what? I can take the bus. Thanks though."

R – Reinforce

Make sure the other party knows why they should grant your request, or acquiesce to your conditions without a fight. "Because I said so" is not a valid reason. Most people reciprocate naturally. In the teenager example, however, it may not be so natural. Let them know that something's in it for them.

You might say something like this, "You get to stay home from church on the condition that you are productive at home. Since you don't like church and I don't like cooking after church, it's a win for both of us."

Or in the example with the car, it might sound like this, "I actually need to drive to a different city for a few days, but I can't rent a car because of (XYZ), so I'll get your car diagnosed for you, and if I can afford to fix the overheating problem, I will. If not, I'll see if anyone else can part with their car for a few days, or find another solution."

In both examples, the other party can clearly see that they have nothing to lose by accepting your request, and everything to gain.

This is important because relationships are built on reciprocity. When one party feels slighted occasionally, it's not a big deal. But if one party feels slighted more often than not, they will most likely end the relationship.

M – *Mindful (stay)*

Stay focused on the conversation. If you're answering a text, they have no reason to listen to you. If they're answering a text, that's out of your control, but you can keep your mind on the conversation instead of what they're doing. If they become defensive, notice what you may have said wrong, apologize if necessary, even if it's just to get them back on track.

This is important because it's too easy to go off track and lose focus, especially in an uncomfortable situation, where the other party might be looking to pick a fight. If you go off on tangents, whether they be to sing and dance because some said a song lyric, or to fight, or because one of you saw a squirrel, you have less of a chance of getting what you want. Especially if you're the one singing and dancing or chasing squirrels.

Let's go back to the hypothetical teenager.

Your teen may interrupt you to tell you that they've been cutting church every week with their friends from Sunday School anyway, so there's no point in going. You may have to repeat yourself a few times, especially if you're letting them stay home as long as they're productive, as they may not believe their ears.

Again, repeat yourself as often as necessary, and if you have a real kid, you've done that a few times already this morning. And bring the conversation back to the topic. Detour… focus. If we're using the example of asking an adult friend for something, you don't have the clout you do as a parent. You still may have to repeat yourself, but the interruptions might just be singing and dancing.

You might say something like, "I understand you don't like church, and you cut Sunday School anyway. But you get some out of it every week if you continue going, and I would like that." Or, "If you're going to stay home, you'll need to cook for us, and I'll take the added precaution of changing the Wi-Fi password every Saturday to make sure you'll be productive. If you can prove that you are, that you don't have friends over, that you cook and clean as you go, I'll stop doing that."

A – *Appear Confident*

Appear confident no matter how you actually feel. If you have this look all the time, little old ladies will ask you for a napkin at a restaurant when you're on a date, and it might not even occur to you to tell them you don't work there, so you walk into the kitchen and get the napkins.

Your nonverbal cues indicate confidence more than your verbal cues. Sit with your back straight and your head held high. Make eye contact. Orient your feet towards them. Where your feet are oriented is where your mind subconsciously goes. Appear confident and stand your ground.

This is important because confidence signifies that your request isn't too difficult to grant and that you're harder to turn down. There's no need to be overbearing like Ferris Bueller. If they do refuse you, in an adult to adult conversation, you might just ask if they're sure, then thank them for their time and let it go.

If our teenager refuses you, this might be a good time to tell them what the other option is. "Okay, you don't have to learn to cook. And if you can read, you can cook, by the way. You can keep coming to church with us, and thank you for letting me know about cutting Sunday School. I'll be sure to tell your friends' parents you all do that because they'll want to know too. I'll let them know you told me. Thank you for caring about the salvation of your friends, who also should go back to church." This will most likely ensure you an excellent meal every Sunday.

N – *Negotiate*

Negotiate. Remember, "give to get", as selfish as that sounds. Everyone wonders, *What's in it for me*? You aren't demanding something. You're asking for something or setting down a rule. Even in setting down rules, you aren't demanding. If you think you can demand something of someone, even a child, expect defensiveness and confrontation. You give options.

You may need to alter your request to make it more pleasing. In the borrowing the car example, you offered to get the car diagnosed (AutoZone does it for free) and fix it if you could – and if you couldn't, you'd find another solution to our problem.

This is important because building relationships may or may not be the most important reason we spend a few decades on this planet, but it certainly takes up most of our time. Whether we spend that time in actual relationships with other human beings or wondering why we drive away other human beings, we spend an inordinate amount of time either with other people or thinking about them, whether we know them personally or not.

So if we spend our energy browbeating others and expecting them to kowtow to us, that only works if you have money, and even then not everyone likes you, even if you somehow win elections. Mere mortals, without insane amounts of money, can't behave like that. We have to negotiate and play nice.

Going back to the example of the teenager, this is pretty much already a negotiation. They still refuse to go to church or cook, and they tell you they don't care if you call their friends' parents. They really do. This is when you pull out your phone and look up the numbers of the kids' parents, who you probably know, at least by name already. Google white pages are great. Some rules are not to be negotiated. If, however, you start the conversation with trying to force them to go to church, this idea is a perfect negotiation, and now it seems (to them) that you've given in some.

But for example's sake, you do try to negotiate. You might say, "Okay, if you don't come to church with us on Sunday, you still need to be productive at home. Would you rather have a list of chores to do? What is your suggestion to being productive, other than homework, because I don't want you deliberately putting it off until Sunday?"

This approach helps your child feel like they have a say – like their voice is heard and not invalidated. If you start off demanding they go, then negotiate to this, you can offer it as a suggestion, and ask which of your suggestions they like best.

You can both leave the conversation feeling like you've accomplished something, like you've got a win, like you're helping the other person out, with no ill will.

D.E.A.R. M.A.N.

Using the DEAR MAN skills will improve any relationship. Start now. If you're yelling at each other all the time, at least you're still talking; there's still hope. It's when you've stopped talking entirely that it's harder to reconcile. These skills can reduce arguments and improve understanding. Let's put the whole conversation together now.

Describe: "I've noticed you don't like church. Let's discuss the options of staying home."

Express: "I feel like you should believe what I believe, but I know that you're your own person, separate from me, and I can't force my beliefs on you. I would like you to come to church with us because my worry is that you won't be productive at home."

Assert: "I understand that you don't want to come to church with us, and you are old enough to stay home alone. So, if you choose to stay home instead of attending church, you will prepare dinner and set the table and have everything prepared for us to be able to eat when we return, and you will make enough in case we invite people over unexpectedly. If you are unable to complete this chore, and thus, be productive for the whole family while we are at church, you will come back with us, even if you don't believe it."

Reinforce: "You get to stay home from church on the condition that you are productive at home. Since you don't like church and I don't like cooking after church, it's a win for both of us."

Mindful (stay): "I understand you don't like church, and you cut Sunday School anyway. But you get some out of it every week if you continue going, and I would like that." Or, "If you're going to stay home, you'll need to cook for us, and I'll take the added precaution of changing the Wi-Fi password every Saturday to make sure you'll be productive. If you can prove that you are, that you don't have friends over, that you cook and clean as you go, I'll stop doing that."

Appear Confident: "Okay, you don't have to learn to cook. And if you can read, you can cook, by the way. You can keep coming to church with us, and thank you for letting me know about cutting Sunday School. I'll be sure to tell your friends' parents you all do that because they'll want to know too. I'll let them know you told me. Thank you for caring about the salvation of your friends, who also should go back to church."

Negotiate: "Okay, if you don't come to church with us on Sunday, you still need to be productive at home. Would you rather have a list of chores to do? What is your suggestion to being productive, other than homework, because I don't want you deliberately putting it off until Sunday?"

Using Relationship Effectiveness (G.I.V.E.)

GIVE is the DBT acronym used for obtaining and maintaining relationships. This is difficult for many people, but more so with people living with mental illnesses.

G – (be) Gentle

Be kind when addressing people. It seems we're much more capable of being kind to complete strangers and people we work with (but don't really like) than people we actually love. If you have a difficult topic to address with a loved one, be conscious of your tone of voice, facial expressions, body posture, and other nonverbal cues we all send every day.

Be able to take NO for an answer from the DEAR MAN approach. Again, this is a conversation between adults and not your hypothetical child. They have every right to say no without being guilted, judged, manipulated, or begged.

Don't leave the discussion or threaten or manipulate them. Don't threaten to hurt them or someone else or yourself. If you're truly feeling the need to self-harm when talking with them, apologize for trying to start this discussion, leave the situation, and seek help.

Don't name call, condescend, bring up past injuries or "debts" you think they owe you. They do not owe you the right to say yes, no matter what you've done in the past. If this is a one-sided relationship, you may want to reevaluate how much time and energy you invest in it. Don't guilt trip or force the issue.

Thank them for their time. Leave the situation or change the subject at an appropriate time. Remember this: no one owes you anything, and you don't owe anyone anything. Be kind. Use your inside voice, and go right on back to being friends after they say no. You're an adult. You can solve this problem.

I – (act/be) Interested

The manual says to act interested in what the other person has to say; however, you should instead *be* interested. Anyone can act interested. You're probably acting interested now, reading this. But in discussions with loved ones, especially difficult discussions, the kind that a DEAR MAN approach necessitates, you need to be interested. They're going to say something that may be important in a later conversation.

Be interested. Be present. Be mindful. Show them the same interest you would like shown. Don't invalidate their words by your words or actions (or inactions or silence). Let them feel heard. Really listen to what they're saying, instead of waiting to speak. Worse yet, don't interrupt them to speak.

Ask open-ended questions that show you're actually listening. Pay attention to your body language and make sure it's inviting and also showing interest, like nodding. Maintain eye contact. When you do speak, make sure you're not speaking only about yourself. Make space for other people in the conversation. Be comfortable with silence. Really, it's okay.

Be cognizant of the other person's needs. If they wish to discuss something else, make sure this topic is done, and both parties feel satisfied. If you're not there yet, let them know you're happy to discuss it at another time.

V – Validate

Allow the other person to feel what they feel. Don't tell them how they should or shouldn't feel. Don't tell them they're just talking like a debater when they make good points – as if that fact invalidates their argument. Don't dismiss what they have to say because they're younger than you or because they haven't had your experiences.

Let them know you understand where they're coming from, even if you don't agree with their point. "I totally understand why you think that now. Thank you for explaining it like that. I still don't agree, but I'll stop trying to change your mind on the matter."

Try to determine what part of your request the other person is uncomfortable with. "I know you're busy, but I'm not in a rush." Or, "I didn't know your car was such a piece of crap, and that's why you work from home. I'll figure out a way to rent a car."

Even without conflict, this is an important interpersonal skill to learn. Everyone likes to feel validated and heard. Everyone likes to know they matter in a relationship. Validating other people is one of the most necessary facets in relationships of trust.

E – (use an) Easy Manner

Smiling goes a long way in conversations with or without conflict. Not the forced, "I actually want to kill you" smile, but a real one. Unless you've worked in customer service for upwards of a decade, that smile always looks fake. If you have, you're a natural. You can give fake smiles to the best human lie detectors around.

A little humor goes a long way too. If you tell a joke and it falls flat, blame it on your dad. "That was one of my dad's worst dad jokes. Actually, it might have been his best. He's an accountant." If you say something serious and they all look at you weird, then you were kidding. "I'm kidding! When you look at me like that, I'm kidding!"

Offer a sincere compliment. If you can't think of one, tell them you're jealous of their clean criminal background. If you don't have a follow-up story for why you'd say that, you were kidding. When they look at you like that, you were kidding. Lighten up the situation with a little self-deprecating humor. Really, that stuff is the best. If nothing else, just smile and nod and give them a little more attention. Make them feel special.

Self-Respect Effectiveness (F.A.S.T.)

F.A.S.T. is about maintaining self-respect during conflicts. You may have had the role of doormat for way too long. You may have the role of the youngest, the "baby", and thus, always treated as such, no matter how old you are. Set healthy boundaries, even late in the game. Maintain your self-respect. This is possible even with the self-deprecating humor if you've set healthy boundaries. You'll want to use these skills in sequential order, then altogether.

F – Fair

Be fair to yourself and others. Those with borderline personality disorder usually also have anxiety and depression (mental illnesses are like potato chips – you can't have just one). One of anxiety's favorite past times is to make every decision, action, reaction, everything that happens, completely catastrophic, apocalyptic, no coming back. It's great fun. Here's a little trick. Name your anxiety. Use a fictional character you hate. If you use a real person you hate, it'll increase your anxiety. When you get these crazy end of the world scenarios building up, say, "Umbridge, go away." Or whatever you named it. That helps to separate yourself from the anxiety and helps you recognize *you're* not freaking out – your anxiety is.

Be fair in both thoughts and actions. Instead of thinking the other person is the worst person on the planet, or you're the dumbest person ever born, redirect your thoughts to something fairer, then focus on the subject again. Find the elements of truth in their argument. Ask clarifying questions if you can't. Get to a point where their argument makes sense to you. You don't have to agree with it, but now you understand it, and you may even agree with elements of it.

A – (no) Apologies

This isn't to say don't apologize when you're in the wrong. When you're in the wrong, absolutely apologize. This isn't to say don't apologize when you're not in the wrong. A common example of this is a typical woman. She'll say "Sorry" as she passes you instead of "Excuse me," or "On your left."

When you're resolving a conflict with someone, you might be tempted to apologize just to get it over with and accept blame when it doesn't belong to you. Maintain your dignity. Don't do this. Don't even offer a fake "I'm sorry you feel that way" apology. Offer a "Why do you feel that way?" or a "What responsibilities do you think you have in this scenario?" open-ended question without appointing blame or getting defensive.

S – Stick to Your Values

To stick to your values, you first have to know *what* your values are. Determine your values before opening this dialogue. Do some introspective self-examination and figure out what's important to you, what you won't bend on, and what you can bend on without losing any respect for yourself. The only person who HAS to live in your head is you. Make sure that is a person you can respect and love. Be honest about what you say your values are, and what they actually are. If you say you value fiscal responsibility but never budget, you need to either start budgeting or stop saying you value fiscal responsibility. If you say you value family but cheat on your wife, reevaluate yourself. It might help to write down your values then write down the actions you do that would corroborate those values. This might help you to determine your values. After you know what you stand for, keep standing.

T – (be) Truthful

Be truthful with yourself and others. Do you downplay your accomplishments and exaggerate your faults? So you downplay or avoid your faults entirely and exaggerate your accomplishments? Do you take credit or blame when it belongs to someone else? In the adult world, there is no need for this. You will be viewed as more honest among others if you can be honest with yourself. Are your words true? Will your version of a story closely match other people's? Are you as objective as possible about yourself and others?

Using these steps will allow you to maintain your dignity. You may not be pleased with the outcome of the discussion, but you can walk away with your head held high.

T.H.I.N.K.

These are the basics of Dialectical Behavior Therapy. Using these steps will help in interpersonal relationships with or without conflict. There is a newer acronym, not widely known, but it is useful in interactions with conflict. It's called THINK, and its purpose is to help you reduce negative emotions towards others.

T – Think

Think about the situation from all angles. Think about it from the other person's point of view. Try to step into their shoes. Do they view you as unreasonable as perhaps you view them? Listen to the words coming out of your own mouth with an objective mind.

H – Have empathy

This is where you really try to walk around in their shoes, as Atticus Finch would say. What else is going on in their lives that might make them behave like this? Their behavior towards you might not be entirely about you. What does it feel like to be them? Let yourself feel their emotions for a moment.

I – Interpretations

Interpret and misinterpret their behavior. Try to figure out why they might be behaving this way. Start with outlandish ideas to firstly open your mind, and secondly, realize how outlandish it sounds so you can come close to what might be a reality. For example, you might start out with this assumption and lead yourself to less outlandish ones:

She's a test subject to see how mean she can be and is getting paid for this behavior. She's a test object to see how mean people can be to her, but it's a double-blind study, so she doesn't know why she's getting paid or why a particular person is horrible to her, and she's reacting to that. She's not involved with any tests about meanness but just enjoys doing it for free. Her kid got called to the principal's office again, and she's sick of missing work for him and doesn't know what she's doing wrong. She's tired and having a bad day, bad week. I should just tell her she's doing a great job and not let it get to me.

The point of that exercise is to bring your anger down enough to be able to do the next two steps.

N – Notice

Notice the other person. Notice if he or she looks tired instead of angry. Notice if he or she has a lot on their plate. Notice if you are inadvertently adding more. Notice if they smile at you, even if you're not on good terms. Hopefully, you smile back, but you don't have to do anything just yet. Just notice.

K – Kindness

This doesn't mean forgive and forget. This doesn't mean that if they apologize, you can go back to treating them poorly – nor can they do that to you. It just means be kind. You may need your space for a bit. Instead of saying, "Leave me alone! I don't want to talk to you!" try saying, "What you said really hurt, and I need some time to process it – so I need some space for a little bit, please." This will give you a much better response, and when you're ready to talk to them again, they'll be more willing to express in a civil manner why they said what they said or did what they did – and maybe they'll apologize, and maybe they won't. In the end, what's important is they will have nicer feelings towards you.

This skill set could be determined as an interpersonal distress skill set. Like all the acronyms we've discussed, you won't become a master of any of these overnight. They all require daily practice and self-reflection.

There's one more thing to add to this extensive list of improving interpersonal relationships. It's not an acronym, and it's not found in any text read during a master's degree in interpersonal communications.

It's **T.H.A.N.K.** Just thank the other person for something every day. It might be small. It might be something they should do because they live there, too. If, for example, your husband takes out the trash every day, start thanking him. If your wife is a stay-at-home mom, start thanking her for the million thankless things she does every day. A simple act of gratitude will get you far, even just something like, "Hey, I don't know what your job entails, but I know it's hard – so thanks for letting me work. Thanks for keeping the kids alive and fed every day."

Conclusion

Dialectical behavior therapy has offered much in the realm of therapies. Dr. Linehan has saved thousands of lives with her innovative work. A borderline personality disorder is not being "crazy" or "unhinged". It's simply a mental illness. It includes many other mental illnesses as facets of it. Because of that, it only makes sense that an effective therapy would include many types of therapy and self-reflection.

Mindfulness is probably the most important aspect of DBT because we have been trained not to be mindful. We're like ants, scurrying around – hurry, hurry, hurry, but going nowhere.

Mindfulness forces you to focus on the present. Ask yourself, "Am I treading water? Am I at the bottom of a rung I do want to be on or the middle of one I don't?" When you choose mindfulness, you look at your life for a moment.

Your questions aren't all going to be answered in one moment of mindfulness. It's something that must be practiced every day. DBT is an excellent medium for learning skills of mindfulness and interpersonal relationships. When therapy is complete, you've acquired an outstanding toolkit of skills to reach from in any situation.

Our entire lives are our memories and our interpersonal relationships. Because DBT focuses on mindfulness and interpersonal relationships, it is one of the most effective types of therapies. When we're mindful, we're creating memories. We're technically creating memories when we're not mindful as well – but not memories of what's actually happening.

In summary, by practicing the skills of DBT, we create memories and interpersonal relationships. And having good memories and relationships is what makes a life worth living.

Check out more books by Steven Turner

EMPATH

*Your Guide to Understanding Empaths and
Their Emotional Abilities to Feel Empathy,
Including Tips for Highly Sensitive People, Dealing
with Energy Vampires, and Being a Psychic Empath*

Steven Turner

DARK PSYCHOLOGY

What Machiavellian People of Power Know about Persuasion, Mind Control, Manipulation, Negotiation, Deception, Human Behavior, and Psychological Warfare that You Don't

Steven Turner

Made in United States
Orlando, FL
07 December 2022